MY RED MONKEY AND OTHER CHILDHOOD MEMORIES

A Memoir by Barbara Winther

Cover art by Lynn Cooper

Interior design by Michael Smith

ISBN: 1723023108
ISBN: 978-1723023101

Other Books By Barbara Winther

Carter Crab

Ralph's Dream

Nobody but the Wind

The Time of the Kachinas

The Tiger Drums

The Leopard Sings

The Jaguar Dances

Let It Go Louie—Croatian Immigrants on Puget Sound

They Like Noble Causes

Hopitu

Plays from Hispanic Tales

Plays from Asian Tales

Plays from African Tales

Plays from Folktales of Asia and Africa

For My Husband Grant, My Son Mikael, and
His Wife Cheryl

Acknowledgments

Thank you to Robin of Island Care Givers. To Cheryl Johnson for editing help. To my writer's group, Brett, Larry, and especially Mike Smith, who completed the publication process when I was no longer able to do so. And to Lynn Cooper for my cover art.

WASHINGTON, D.C.

According to my birth certificate, I was born as Barbara Jane Hunter in 1926 at Garfield Hospital in Washington D. C. My first four years were spent in that city, mostly in the large front bedroom at 1537 Monroe Street. I've never forgotten that address. Perhaps it was drilled into me in case I wandered off and got lost. I lived there with my mother's mother, my grandma, who had legal guardianship of me. She owned a tea room someplace in Washington, using elegant cups and plates hand painted with pink roses, green leaves, and gold trim. I still have two preserved in a china cabinet.

The Monroe Street home belonged to my father's parents, Grandmother and Granddaddy Hunter. It was a brick row house, looking pretty much like the group of six or eight other brick houses attached to it. Three cement steps led from the sidewalk to a wide front porch, where in the summer rummy games were played every night except Sunday. The entry hall of the house had a stairway that led up to two bedrooms, a screened back porch, where Grandmother and Granddaddy Hunter slept when it was too hot, and the bathroom with a big claw-foot tub and a toilet that flushed by yanking a chain on the tank above it.

I don't remember much about the downstairs except for three things: Granddaddy's desk, at which he often sat, tucked under the stairs, a fireplace in the living room, and a large, dark, heavy table in the dining room. I remember the table not because we ate at it—except for celebrations we were served in our room—but because once I was told to dance on it and sing my favorite song: "You're the cream in my coffee. I'm the salt in your stool." Years later I learned my word "stool" should have been "stew." But at the time I thought they were smiling and asking me to do it over again because my dancing in circles was good and my singing, especially on the last word, was loud.

What made early memories stick with me? Were they events I considered terribly important? A fear? An accident? Were they brought to mind through a photo? By Grandma's account of what happened? All were contributing factors. Hard to figure out which were actual memories. So I've thrown them together into the slow-cooker of *childhood memories.*

The earliest ones I can pull out happened in Washington, D. C. I sat in a baby carriage going down a busy sidewalk, probably 16th Street, clutching a can of spaghetti. Perhaps Grandma had just bought it. A lady with a blue feather on her hat looked in at me and said "Well, well, what do you have there?" I replied, "Getti." Even today, I can see that lady peering in at me.

While I was learning to walk, I attempted to climb the screen on someone's porch that was shaded by trees from a nearby park. I suppose I thought I might be able to reach the park that way. I got halfway up the screen and started screaming. I was stuck—couldn't climb higher or lower myself down without falling. A stranger with large hands rescued me.

At the Monroe Street home I drove my tricycle off the front porch and burst into tears because blood flowed out of the front of my head. Beulah, the Hunter's black maid, rushed outside and picked me up. "Honey chile, what you done to yourself?" Pressing her dishtowel against my forehead she whisked me upstairs and into a tub of warm water, her solution to anything wrong with me.

Then, there was the afternoon I experimented with Grandma's lipstick, drawing it all over my face and on the top of her dressing table. Grandma got angry with me not because of my decorations but because I used up her favorite tube. "And lipstick is expensive," she informed me.

A folding screen shut off the dressing table and part of the bed from the rest of the bedroom, so that it was more like a living room. The primary piece of furniture in it was the large, free-standing radio. I think it was a Philco. I sat in front of it on a footstool (I still have it) and listened to *Amos and Andy*. Grandma always laughed when the Kingfish said something, so I laughed too. Also, we listened to a Kate Smith program. She always sang "God Bless America" with such a loud, full voice that it made me think she really meant it. A large upholstered chair reserved for Grandma sat under a bank of windows overlooking a vacant lot across the street. A drop-front desk was on the wall and next to it a single bed covered with a heavy spread that felt and looked like it should be hung on a wall.

What I remember most about the room were the two framed pictures—they may have been prints, but to me they were wonderful paintings. Above the desk was the face and shoulders of a laughing gypsy; above the single bed, a long, dreamy scene of women wearing gauzy clothes lounging by a pool of water. Often, I stared at both pictures and imagined having conversations with the gypsy and lounging by the pool with the ladies.

In the evenings I sat up in bed and looked at pictures in *My Book House*, volumes 1-6, and the three taller books that came with the set—*Nursery Friends from France, Tales Told in Holland*, and my favorite *Little Pictures of Japan*. When Grandma read me a story from *My Book House*, I always asked her to end up reading a couple of poems from the Japanese book. I loved the pictures that went with them.

I had a best friend when I was two years old—Teddy. She lived someplace on Monroe Street. In the summer at night we would often run up and down the street catching fireflies in bottles. We played hide-and-go-seek among the many stairs to basements of the row houses. We had contests, seeing who could spit watermelon seeds the farthest. In the winter when there was snow, Teddy brought out her sled and pushed me down the hill on the vacant lot across the street. When the ice man delivered a huge ice block for our kitchen fridge, using big tongs to carry it, he always ended up giving us each a shaved piece of ice to suck.

One spring when the cherry blossoms were in bloom, Granddaddy Hunter took me down to the pool in front of Lincoln's Memorial to see them. I'm not sure how we got there. Probably by streetcar, as it would have been too far to walk and nobody on the street owned a car. We did, however, walk to Meridian Park, situated on a hill overlooking the Capitol. The most exciting sights there were waterfalls that cascaded down the stairs. Since we only visited the park in the daytime, I could only imagine how beautiful they must have looked at night all lit up.

I don't think my mother and father ever lived together. They got married because my mother was pregnant with me; both were 18 at the time. My father, Daniel Hunter, was studying to be an engineer at George Washington University. I rarely saw him. His appearances were like magic. Once he took me on a ride in the rumble-seat of his new Ford roadster. Another time, I sat in his lap in the open cockpit of an airplane flying over Washington, D.C. The pilot was a friend of my father's. He kept yelling, "Look at the Monument." "Look at the Capitol." "There's Lincoln's Memorial." But I couldn't see a thing because the wind blew so hard I kept my eyes shut.

I don't know why my mother, Virginia Tracy (she took back her maiden name) gave me up to her mother—my grandma. Perhaps Virginia didn't want the responsibility or felt she was too young to handle a baby. Or she might have felt that since she knew nothing about her father, and her mother gave her up when she was a child, why shouldn't she give me up?

That theory goes back to 1908 when Grandma's first husband, Fred Tracy, left her at the time my mother was born. For six years Grandma tried to survive by mending and ironing clothes. The money she received for her work barely covered her bills. Realizing she needed a better means of support, Grandma entered a nurse's training school in Lewiston, Maine, where you had to be unmarried and couldn't have children. She appealed to relatives to take Virginia until she completed her training and could make enough money to give her adequate care. Fred Tracy's two single sisters, Betty and Judith, who lived together in San Francisco, were embarrassed by their brother's desertion. They agreed to take Virginia. However, several months after she arrived, the aunts realized they didn't want to be responsible for raising a child. They placed my mother in a local Catholic school where she lived for the next seven years.

From the start, she caused all sorts of trouble—not obeying school rules, making funny faces at the nuns, climbing out the window for a rendezvous with a boy, and holding secret meetings after lights out to gorge on cookies stolen from the kitchen. The aunts didn't tell Grandma about any of these problems. Instead, they told her that only in a Catholic school could a child get well suited for life.

Meanwhile, after 27 months Grandma finished her training and became an RN (registered nurse). She then found a job in Boston at the Massachusetts Central Hospital. The starting wage was modest, and since Virginia seemed to be doing well at the Catholic school, Grandma decided to wait until she could have more to offer her.

On a particularly cloudy fall afternoon a good-looking man by the name of Compton W. Jones, a well-to do tax accountant, arrived to visit one of Grandma's patients—a banker who had gotten into an argument in a bar. The banker confided in Grandma, whispering, "My brother-in-law punched me in the nose and hit me over the head with a beer bottle." He grimaced as if reliving the event. "I was in the wrong place at the wrong time, talking to the wrong person. Heaven help me if anyone at the bank finds out about this."

When Compton appeared, Grandma, thinking he might have banking connections, told him to go away. She said her patient couldn't have any visitors.

"But he's my best friend," said Compton. "I was with him when he got smashed."

"I'll tell him you were here," she said, refusing to let him in.

Compton was so impressed by her stalwart stand and captivated by her looks, that he asked her for a date. She refused. He came back the next day and waited for her in the parking lot. Again she refused. However, the third time, when he appeared with a dozen red roses, she laughed and said, "I guess you're worth a cup of coffee. Meet me in the cafe across the street."

It was a whirlwind romance. Compton proposed three months later when they attended the Massachusetts 1919 governor's ball for Calvin Coolidge, later the President of the United States. Grandma wore a black sequined dress to the ball. It must have been a memorable time for her because she kept the dress all through her years carefully wrapped in tissue paper. Now it resides, still wrapped in tissue, in a fine old walnut steamer trunk in our front hallway.

Not long after she married Compton, Grandma brought her daughter to Boston, but the damage had been done. Virginia never liked Compton and rebelled against any sort of rules. She claimed Compton sexually assaulted her. Grandma never believed the story. "It just wasn't in Compton to do such a thing," she later told me. And because Grandma didn't believe it happened, neither did I.

However, it couldn't have been a happy marriage. My mother often barricaded herself in the attic, refusing to eat until she got her way. Grandma was constantly in tears over the relationship. Two years later, Compton died of a heart attack. He was found sitting at a desk pouring over tax accounts during one of my mother's tirades.

Grandma never forgave herself for his death. For the rest of her life, she insisted everyone call her Mrs. Compton W. Jones, rather than Grace Jones. "It's the memory of him I want to keep," she said many times.

Compton's death left Grandma with a good deal of money in the stock market. Some of it she used to buy a tea room in Washington D. C., pouring all of her time and energy into it.

At the age of 17, my mother led her own life, unrestricted. She met my father at a party and soon got pregnant with me.

Was the reason why my mother didn't want me because she felt that her mother didn't want her? Did Grandma take legal guardianship of me because she felt it was a second chance to raise a child? I don't know. Neither my mother nor my grandmother ever talked about it. Not until I was grown up did I learn that Grandma had been adopted, her mother dying in childbirth and her father unknown. As for my feelings about the matter, my grandmother or *Bammover* as I called her when I started to speak—*Bam* for short—was always my loving mother to me.

I visited my real mother several times in those early years. She lived on a street in Washington D. C. that sounded like "Sigsbee Place." Not sure if that was the correct name. In one visit I watched my mother paint the outside of her claw-foot bathtub purple. Another time she made an old-fashioned dress for me, complete with pantaloons and a cardboard fabric-covered hat. When the outfit was finished, she dressed me in it and took me to a photographer to have my picture taken. I still have that hand-tinted photograph as well as a snapshot she took of me holding a fuzzy Easter bunny. I never relaxed around my mother, feeling more like an exhibit than a daughter. I was always relieved when it was time to go home to Monroe Street and my beloved *Bammover.*

By the time I was four years old, in 1930, my grandma had lost all her money in the Wall Street tumble. During the Depression, she had to sell her tea room at a loss. No longer could she pay the rent for our bedroom at Monroe Street. Appealing to who I later learned was the brother of her adopted mother, she accepted his offer to come to Maine to live free in a cabin on an island in a lake.

Grandma packed up our clothes, as well as my books and dolls. She made arrangements to ship her desk, upholstered chair, footstool and the laughing gypsy picture. After a tearful goodbye to Grandmother and Granddaddy Hunter, Teddy, and Monroe Street, we took the train to Augusta, Maine, where Grandma's Uncle Bodge picked us up in his horse-drawn buggy and drove us to his farm at Fayette Corners, situated beside Echo Lake.

ON AN ISLAND IN MAINE

Frank Bodge, my great uncle, the brother of my grandma's birth mother, had a farm in the small town of Fayette Corners, Maine. The farm, bordering the eastern shore of Echo Lake, was called "The Twin Barns Farm." One barn was for the cows and the other for hay, a wagon, and Betsy, a draft horse.

My great uncle had two ladies living with him: Great Aunt Lydia, his wife, and Great Aunt Herrick, Grandma's birth father's sister. I loved these elderly ladies, especially because they made little blueberry cakes for me.

In looking over old files, I found Grandma's birth and adoption papers. They reveal that Grace M. Herrick, my grandma, was a child of Greenleaf C. Herrick and Lillian Herrick, born on December 12, 1889. Lillian died in childbirth, and when Grace was eight years old, her father agreed she could be adopted by Oscar F. and Louise S. Neal of Livermore. The Neals were distantly related to the Herrick family, cousins I believe.

In her early years, Grace went to school at Fayette Corners, and most likely was born there. I have a letter from her teacher, Claribel Higgins Gordon (Mrs. Vinton D. Gordon), who in 1951 was the Town Clerk and Treasurer at Livermore Falls, Maine. Grandma had written to the courts to get a birth certificate. However, no records were available before 1900. Claribel wrote back, *Dear Grace, Probably the name on this letterhead doesn't mean a thing to you, but when you were about 10 years old, I was your teacher at Fayette Corners, and I remember you distinctly.*

My grandma raised me, had legal guardianship of me, my mother and father having been divorced and taken off to other places and interests. When I was about four and up until age eight (around 1930-34), we lived on one of the two islands at the south end of Echo Lake near the Bodge farm. Our cabin was on the bigger island, which was about a mile long; the much smaller island we called Loon Island because a couple of loons always nested there.

The first trip to the island, Uncle Bodge packed our trunks and suitcases into the rowboat. I refused to get in with them, crying and trying to run away. I was sure the boat would sink, and I would drown. Not until

Uncle Bodge rowed our things over to the island, left them on the dock, and came back alive did I agree to get into the boat. Even then, I held on tight to Grandma because she assured me she could swim.

Since our cabin had no electricity, we used kerosene lanterns. We had no plumbing; the water pump was in front of the cabin and the outhouse in back. One of my jobs every morning was to empty the chamber pot. I had to balance it carefully, since we slept in the loft reached by a ladder. The front and back porches were screened in, which made it nice on hot days because we could have the doors open for a breeze and not worry about mosquitoes eating us up.

Grandma ironed with an old flat iron she heated on top of the wood cooking stove. Every fall, Great Uncle Bodge delivered several rowboat loads of fire wood, enough to get us through the winter if we were frugal, and we had to be.

Starting at age seven, I attended a one-room school. In wintertime I used snowshoes to get there, and it took me over an hour. When weather was bad, Grandma kept me home. Once in a while Great Uncle Bodge gave me an armful of wood for the school stove. As I remember, all the students took turns doing this.

Every spring Chester Hewett cut blocks of ice from the lake for our sawdust floored cellar (our refrigerator), entered outside with a big narrow door that covered the steps leading down under the cabin. After Chester came, Grandma tested the surface of the lake's ice every day to make sure it was stable enough to walk on to shore. There were usually a few weeks while the ice was cracking up that I couldn't go to school. It was always a big celebration when we could pull the rowboat out into the water and paddle to shore. In my mind I saw myself doing the rowing, but when I see photos of how little I was and how large the rowboat was, I think Grandma must have done the rowing at least until I was eight years old.

After the weather warmed up, on Sundays Grandma wore her beautiful, fashionable irregular hem length, chiffon, flower-print dress, and we held a church service, sitting on a bench at a little point extending out toward the shore. She would read from the Bible. We would sing a hymn, repeat the Lord's Prayer, and that was it! Often on Sunday evenings, a couple of bats flew into our loft and flapped around, keeping us awake. When that happened, we moved to the back porch and slept on the table. Grandma thought the bats visited us because morning ringing of church bells in the town of Kent's Hill chased the bats from the belfry. I wondered where the bats hid during the daytime and why they picked on us. Grandma said bats always had lots of secrets they never shared.

We had a portable phonograph, the windup kind with a big horn. On many summer evenings we put it in the boat and rowed out to the middle of the lake to play Rudy Vale records. Grandma loved to hear his voice echoing over the water. Mother must have visited us one summer, although I have no recollection of it, but there's a photograph of her in the boat with the phonograph. She's wearing a two-piece swim suit and has a scarf tied fashionably around her head.

Once I took all my dolls and the red monkey down to the boat so they could enjoy the music. After we rowed ashore I wanted Grandma to help me carry my dolls back to the cabin, which was set about 50 feet from the water on a slight hill. Grandma said, "You took them down, you bring them up."

"That's not fair," I cried.

I marched the dolls up to the cabin in two loads. Then I stood in front of my grandmother with my hands on my hips and yelled, "I'm as mad as a hornet."

What was Grandma's answer? She burst into laughter, which made me even angrier. For the rest of the afternoon, I stayed up in the tree next to the cabin with Downy, my imaginary playmate. He told me "Life is unfair. Get used to it."

One afternoon I remember seeing a complete eclipse of the sun. It happened while my great aunts were having a party on the farm under the big front yard tree. I was scared and ran away and hid in the horse barn. Another thing I was scared of was the pigsty. A covered shed used to go from the farm house out to the sty so pigs could be reached in the winter without going outside. Sometimes I was asked to feed the pigs, which meant throwing pails of slop off the walkway over the sty. I was afraid that if I fell in, the pigs would eat me.

Great Uncle Bodge was a truck farmer— a wagon farmer in those days. He loaded the wagon with his produce and hitched up Betsy. I rode with him up to Kent's Hill, where he sold his vegetables, milk, bacon, and maybe other pork meat, to a grocer there. The roads were lined with fences made of stone, dug from the earth and stacked up when farms were cultivated.

Some Bodge relatives owned a shop, *Linery and Mantuamaking*, in the nearby town of Livermore Falls. The store sold different kinds of linens and mantuas, a kind of farm dress with a drawstring at the waist. That was before my time, but I had the big wooden sign that once hung outside the building. It is now with the Androscoggin Museum in Augusta.

My grandma's first married name was Tracy, and the Tracy family lived near Fayette. I also sent to the Museum letters from my great, great grandfather, Dr. Daniel S. Tracy, written to his wife when he was a surgeon in the Civil War. He wrote that when he came home he would buy Charlie, his son, a horse, but he died in the war. Daniel received his medical degree from Maine's Bowdoin College. Before the war, from 1841-1860, he practiced medicine in Lewiston.

On a stream not far from the farm was a mill that I believe ground flour. Once I was invited there to a birthday party. Most of the children were older than me and I felt out of place. I remember a three-legged race, where two people with their inner legs tied together in a burlap sack, hobbled forward, around a post and back to the finish line. In the heat of the competition, I fell down and my partner got mad at me. I was so embarrassed I quit playing any more games and was glad to go home.

My only playmate on the island was the imaginary one I called Downy. He lived in the tree next to the cabin. Sometimes he sat cross-legged in the air. He never got mad at me. But once a skunk got on the island, sprayed all over our laundry that Grandma hung out on the clothesline, and she had to bury it all in the ground. Downy told me, "You should have helped your grandma bury the skunk-sprayed clothes." I knew Downy was right. He always was.

One night I went with Uncle Bodge to watch the maple syrup boil down. People brought the syrup they had tapped from their maple trees. All was poured into a big iron kettle over a fire set up under a quickly built lean-to. The people told stories and jokes as they sat around the fire most of the night waiting for the syrup to boil down to sugar. I'm not sure when I fell asleep, but I woke up the next morning at the kitchen table in the Bodge house. Before we went back to the island, Aunt Lydia made me a bowl of hot oatmeal drenched with cream from the morning milking and topped with fresh maple sugar. It was delicious.

The parlor at the Bodge house was seldom used, reserved for in times, such as for visitors or the celebration of special days. Otherwise the curtains were closed to help keep out dust. Once a month the aunts opened the windows for a few hours to air out the room. They dusted the mahogany furniture, and with a carpet sweeper cleaned the large, flower-patterned, hand-hooked rug. The parlor was mostly a forgotten part of the house. Daily living took place in the kitchen.

My most memorable Christmas in Maine was my first one. The day before I went over to the Bodge kitchen to make strings of popcorn, using a large needle and heavy thread. That night Uncle Bodge cut a six-foot fir from his forest and set it up in the middle of the parlor. He and the aunts wound the strings of popcorn around the tree.

Christmas Day it was snowing lightly when we came over from our cabin to celebrate the holiday. We each were given a cup of hot cider to take into the parlor where a cheerful fire was lit in the small fireplace and the magnificent tree awaited us. I was so excited that I didn't watch where I was walking. I tripped on the leg of a chair and fell, spilling my cup of cider onto the beautiful rug. Embarrassed and horrified about what I had done, I burst into tears. Grandma helped me up and led me to the kitchen table where she gave me another cup of hot cider and suggested I stay there. I heard chirps from the aunts as they busied themselves with wet and dry towels, mopping up the damage. Soon Uncle Bodge started singing Joy to the World. The Aunts and Grandma joined in, but I didn't see anything to be joyful about. I pushed aside my cup of cider, lay my hot cheek down on the cool wooden table and cried until the song was over.

The next thing I knew I woke up under a blanket on the couch in the parlor. Grandma was asleep covered by a blanket on the big chair. Coals glowed in the fireplace.

Where was the Christmas tree?

I scrambled up and inspected the rug. No sign of the spilled cider. Had it all been a dream?

I pulled aside one of the window curtains. It was daylight, and the snow had stopped. There was the tree, a light dusting of snowflakes on it. Birds flocked to eat the popcorn.

It hadn't been a dream.

Grandma's voice rose up behind me. "They moved the tree outside after the singing was over. They do that every Christmas. We stayed here last night because the snowdrifts were too large. Uncle Bodge will take us home by sled after breakfast."

She stood and folded up her blanket. "Santa came while you were asleep and left this for you." Reaching down beside her chair, she handed me a large knit stocking chock full of treasures. There were apples and walnuts, two wrapped pieces of fudge and, what was most special, a wonderful, red-furred stuffed monkey. It turned out to be a good Christmas after all.

The third spring I caught a bad cold; it might have been pneumonia. Much of the winter I had been bothered by lung problems. Weeks of coughing, numerous bouts of night wheezing, and many days of difficulties breathing kept me in bed for at least half of January through March. Grandma decided it was time to move to a better climate. "I don't think you can survive another Maine winter," she told me.

I didn't mind not going to school. It was fine by me to stay up in the loft, reading by lantern light the books sent by Granddaddy and Grandmother Hunter. I especially liked *The Jungle Book* by Rudyard Kipling, reading it over and over. I pictured myself along with Downy (my imaginary playmate), and the red-furred monkey (a toy I took to bed every night) sailing up *the great gray green greasy Limpopo River, all set about with fever trees.* We had narrow escapes from crocodiles and made friends with a pack of wolves and a troop of English-speaking monkeys.

Another book I often reread many times was *A Child's Garden of Verses* by Robert Louis Stevenson. My favorite poem was the one about making a camp under the stairs. Only for me it was *up in the loft.*

Then there were three books about Indians on the prairie. I think one of them was called *Red Feather.* In my mind I still see the white covers inset with pictures of an Indian boy at different times of his life. On the third book in the series, a warrior gallops along with his spear held high, ready to be hurled at an enemy or a buffalo.

We made a trip down to Washington sometime during our last winter in Maine, and I was taken to an elementary school and put in a second grade class for three days. I didn't like being in a place with children I didn't know, taught by a gray-haired teacher who carried a wooden wand. She pointed it at students she thought weren't paying attention. I wondered if she might beat a pupil if she thought it necessary.

On the last day in the class, we were gathered on chairs in a circle each of us to read out loud a few paragraphs from a book. The wand touched a boy on the other side of the circle, and he read, stumbling over a couple of words. The wand hit his page and he reread the section. This time he got all the words right. As the wand moved around the circle, coming ever closer to me, I grew more nervous. Unaware of what I was doing, I tore off a corner of each page as I turned it. When the wand reached the girl next to me, I shifted in my chair and the torn-off corners fluttered to the floor. The girl stopped reading. She watched the papers go down. Everyone looked at the bits on the floor.

There was an ominous silence.

The teacher cleared her throat. She stood behind me. Her wand flicked onto my book. "What are you doing, Barbara Jane?"

"Nothing."

"Why did you deface your book?"

"I didn't do it."

"You most certainly did." She grabbed my book and closed it with a thump.

I quivered all over and didn't know what to do. Luckily, the recess bell rang.

The teacher stalked over to the blackboard, raised her wand, and said, "Dismissed."

All of the students except me scrambled to put the books away in their desks. Then they rushed outside.

I picked up the bits of papers and stood up, still trembling, waiting for the wand to descend on me. The teacher walked over and took the corners from my hand. To my surprise she said gently, "You've had a difficult morning. Go outside and play."

Tears of relief in my eyes, I ran out the door.

The girl who sat next to me in the reading circle came up and put an arm around my shoulder. "I don't think you did it," she said.

Of course she knew I had done it, but what a nice thing for her to say.

Some thirty years ago, I went back to Fayette, Maine for a visit. I found out at the general store that the "Twin Barns Farm" was now owned by a couple who only came to it in the summer, and they weren't there yet, but we could have a look around. Also, I learned that Chester Hewett, the ice-cutter, was still alive and got directions to his house. He came to the door in a walker because he'd been hit by a falling tree limb last spring. When I told him who I was, he remembered me. "You're the little girl who was scared of the otters."

I said, "I forgot about that. Well, this is my husband, Grant."

Chester looked him up and down and then said, "What do you do?"

"I'm a lawyer," Grant said.

"Don't much like lawyas," said Chester.

"Neither do I," Grant replied.

Chester cleared his throat. "In that case, you both can come in for a piece of my wife's spice cake and a cup of coffee."

So that's what we did for an hour or so of shared memories. Also he told us where the Bodges were buried.

"Once a month I go there to take care of the weeds," he said. "Guess after I'm gone, those graves'll go to hell, but at least while I'm alive, they'll look mighty good. It's what you do fer yer friends." He looked over at his wife. "We're gettin so old all our friends have died, so nobody'll be left to care fer our graves."

His wife spoke up, "Honey, don't you worry none. We'll be under the ground, so it won't make much difference what's atop of us."

Then his wife told us how to get to the house where my mother was born (we have a painting of that house). "The folks who live there are friendly enough. If you go, be sure to see the little birthin' room. On the table in there's where yer Motha came into this world."

We did pay our respects to the Bodge's gravesites—not a weed around. Then we visited the house and peeked in at the table in the birthing room. All I could think of was it must've been an awfully hard place for Grandma to have a baby.

Later, we climbed over a wire fence beside the farm and talked a man with a boat into taking us out on the lake for a visit to the island. Our cabin had been replaced by a fancy cottage. Nobody was home, but through the side window I saw a refrigerator, a modern cook stove, and an electric lamp on a table. There was no sign of the outhouse in back or the water pump in front, so we figured they must have indoor plumbing.

When we got back to shore, I walked down the now paved road to my little schoolhouse. The stone fences that used to line the road were gone. The schoolhouse now appeared to be a library, not yet open for the summer. I couldn't find the mill although we located the stream that used to run it.

But, I was glad to see that Great Uncle Bodge's farmhouse and both barns were still there. In the rafters of the horse barn I spied the stub of a rope. Tears came to my eyes as I remembered how I used to climb up into the hay loft, grab the rope and swing out of the opening into the wide, wonderfully blue sky.

TO CALIFORNIA

Grandma got a temporary nursing job with the Veteran's Hospital south of San Francisco. She was sure she could get government clearance for a fulltime job. So, off we went by train to California. I don't remember how many times we had to change trains or how many days it took us to get to Oakland. I think it was four or five days. But I do remember sleeping one night in the upper birth with a smelly mustard plaster on my chest. The next morning, Grandma took the mustard plaster off, and the kind old black porter brought a pitcher of hot water for Granma to clean me up.

Remarkably, my chest congestion was gone. I felt great, excited to soon be crossing the prairie, hopeful of seeing Indians and buffalo. Well, when we got there, I didn't see anything except mile after mile of dark, blowing granular dust that pattered against the window pane like tiny fingers trying to get in. Years later I learned that the dust storms were the result of a long drought during which farmers, unable to plant their crops, had to leave their homes and their land, suffering terrible losses. To a seven-year-old girl like me, though, it was merely a disappointment.

Just about every night our passenger car was uncoupled and attached to other cars or a new locomotive. At least I think that was happened, as we got jerked about with lots of banging and squealing sounds that reminded me of Great Uncle Bodge's pigs.

The best times were when we swayed with the train, walking down the aisle and onto the platform. After we left the dust bowl, cold, clean air rushed in on the sides. We heard the clacking of the wheels on the rails and felt the jerking movement of the couplings beneath out feet. We pulled open the heavy door to the dining car. Sparkling white tablecloths, large cloth napkins and a black waiter. Now that I think about it, I didn't see any white folks working inside the trains except for the ticket checker, a different one each day. He made sure we were in the right car and had paid the right price to where we were going.

Crossing the mountains was fun because you went through tunnels and snow sheds. Kind of spooky, though. What would happen if a bunch of snow blocked us from getting out of a tunnel? We'd have to back down the mountain. What if snow blocked both ends of the tunnel? We'd be entombed.

In spite of my fears, we made it safely over two sets of mountains—the Rockies and the Sierras. Down from Donner Summit chugged our train into a green, growing valley and the sunshine of California.

Our train trip ended in Oakland. We then boarded a ferry from the place where a few years later a bridge was built to San Francisco. Watching the city, shrouded in fog, come into focus was like approaching Oz at the end of the yellow brick road.

At the dock we were met by Great Aunt Judy, a heavy lady with a face full of creases. Her hair was a rusty shade of brown with gray roots, mostly tucked under a navy blue cloche. "Grace?" she said coming up to Grandma. "And are you little Barbara Jane?" I nodded vigorously. Of course she knew who we were; I was the only little girl with a grownup to get off the ferry.

Aunt Judy drove us to Jefferson Street in the Marina District, stopping in a car parking area partially surrounded by a stately-looking three-story building. Inside, we climbed a curved stairway to a second floor front apartment. A much thinner great aunt, Betty, waited for us with dinner—a small casserole. It tasted good, and so I asked, "What's in it?"

Aunt Betty replied, "Fresh zucchini and canned artichoke hearts held together with a can of mushroom soup and topped with Velveeta Cheese." She drew herself up with an air of importance. "It's an old standby I serve to all our guests."

The casserole divided into four parts didn't give much to each of us, even less to me, since I was the smallest. "Delicious," I said. Holding up my empty plate, I started to ask for more, but got only as far as "I'd like—" when Grandma cleared her throat and gave me a sharp look. I started again, "I'd... ah...I'd like Grandma to have the recipe," I concluded and set my plate back down.

As the aunts cleared the table to the kitchen, Grandma whispered to me, "Be thankful for what you get. I doubt if they're used to feeding so many people."

After the dishes were washed and put away, the aunts moved back the dining room table and chairs. They pivoted the closet door and miraculously pulled down a made-up double bed. I jumped in right away, tired from the excitement of our arrival in San Francisco. Except on the train trip, Grandma and I always slept together in spoon fashion. It gave me a sense of security and warmth to cuddle up behind my grandma. That night was the best sleep I'd had since leaving the island on Echo Lake.

The next morning, Grandma left by bus to check in on her nursing job. That night she called to say she was staying at the hospital until the weekend, three days away. I spent most of my time reading *Swiss Family Robinson,* a book the aunts had checked out of the library for me. When I wasn't reading, I pretended that I and my red monkey were stuck up in a tree house with wild animals waiting below to eat us. One of the mornings I watched Aunt Judy brush brown dye into the roots of her hair. I was impressed by the fact that although she put a white towel over her shoulders, she didn't drop one bit of brown dye onto it. That afternoon Aunt Betty took me for a walk down the few blocks to the marina to see the boats—lots of them lined up beside the boulevard and the long pier.

It was on the third day that my real mother arrived in her new Chevrolet coupe. "You're going to live with me from now on," she said, scooping up my box of dolls and books and my suitcase of clothes.

"Where are we going?" I asked, alarmed by what was happening.

"To King City," she replied. "Here, put your feet over the box. I'll slip the suitcase in behind your seat."

Aunt Judy yelled through an opened slit in her second floor window, "Wait till Grace comes back."

"No!" snapped my mother. "This is *my* daughter."

Aunt Judy opened the window wider, "Where's King City?"

Mother leaped into the driver's seat and rolled down her window. "A small town below Salinas," she called up.

"Never heard of the place," cried Aunt Judy.

"Get a California map," Mother bellowed and started the engine.

Aunt Judy slammed down her window.

Mother sped to the end of Jefferson Street, rolled up her window, and headed south.

"Will Grandma be living with us?" I asked.

"No."

"How come?"

"Not enough room. We'll be in a trailer."

I swallowed hard. "Then, let's get a bigger place."

"Can't do that."

"Why not?"

She shot me a frown. "That's enough questions. I've got to concentrate on driving."

I folded my arms and shouted, "I hate King City."

The only reaction I got from my mother was a long, heavy sigh.

As we continued driving south, I pulled my red monkey out of the box, curled up with it, and fell asleep.

To drive the approximately 150 miles from San Francisco to King City in 1934 you had to pass through every town along the way. I think I woke up at each stop light. Once, when Mother bought gas, I went to the bathroom at the station. Another time I heard the sad sound of a train whistle and clanging bells and saw a train clatter past. It seemed as if this trip would go on...and on...forever.

KING CITY

The silver trailer was located behind the King City Hospital. Inside, at one end of the trailer were two single beds with a small table between them, a lamp on it. At the other end was a rack with mother's clothes hanging on it, noticeably two white uniforms; beside the rack was a straight-back chair. In the middle of the room, opposite the entry door, was a portable, round electric heater. There were no windows, no cooking facilities, and no bathroom. It didn't seem much like a home to me. Before I could ask any questions, Mother pointed to the left bed, "That one's yours," she said.

I sat down on it, still clutching my red monkey.

She then informed mc I would be using the bathroom at the back of the hospital. "No tub, but there's a shower," she said.

I didn't know anything about a shower. How did a person use such a thing? Did you take all your clothes off and sit down in it? However, I said nothing. Just nodded.

Mother continued, 'I'll bring your meals to you from the hospital."

Again I nodded.

There was a knock on the trailer door. Mother let in a man. "This is the doctor at the hospital," she said. "Don't tell anyone about his visits."

They left the trailer and stood outside talking. After a bit they stopped.

Silence.

The door had been left ajar. Curious about what might be happening, I sneaked over and peered around the edge.

The doctor was kissing my mother.

I rushed over to my bed and crawled under the covers, clutching my red monkey. When my mother at last came back then left, closing and locking the door behind her, I pretended to be asleep.

Mother was a nurse at the hospital. I didn't know she was a real nurse. Once I heard Grandma and Mother arguing—they always argued—about Mother being kicked out of nursing school. Something about having a boy visiting her when he shouldn't. But when I asked Mother, "How'd you get to be a nurse?" she replied, "The same way anyone does. I trained for it."

"But I heard—" I stopped and chewed on my lower lip.

"What did you hear?" Mother asked, her eyes penetrating me.

"Nothing," I replied. "Can I ride my bicycle to school from now on?"

"No. It might get stolen. Besides, it's healthy for you to walk. I got you that bike to ride after school. You get out at three and I get off work at four, so you have a full hour to ride around town. Just stay off Broadway. It's too busy with traffic."

And that was the end of that conversation.

On Easter Sunday the hospital doctor gave me a white rabbit—a real live one. He said, "You'll find it in a hutch at the back of the hospital lot." He handed me a carrot with its green top still on. "I'll bring you the food. Each time you go, spend about an hour with your new pet." He added, "That way, it'll get used to you as its feeder."

I looked at the carrot and then at the doctor, dumfounded, confused, unable to believe what he said could be true.

"That's a wonderful gift," said Mother. "Barbara Jane, what do you say to the doctor?"

I finally found my voice. "Thank you."

Mother smiled. "Good girl. Go along now. Have fun with your rabbit."

I started for the door.

The doctor said, "Be sure to lock the hutch before you leave it."

I opened the door, jumped out over the two steps to the trailer, and ran through the tall grass toward the back of the lot. There, in front of the picket fence was a wooden box with a cage on top, my white rabbit huddled inside. After twisting the metal lock to open the door, I set the carrot down in front of the rabbit. It sniffed the food, eyed me, pulled the carrot toward its mouth, and started to nibble.

I closed the cage, knelt down and sat on the back of my heels. "I'll call you Bunny Boo," I told the rabbit. "Bunny Boo, I love you, yes I do, Bunny Boo." I sang my verse through a second and a third time. I reopened the cage and coaxed my rabbit forward by tugging the carrot to the front. Carefully I picked Bunny Boo up and buried my nose in its thick white fur. Its heart beat fast against my cheek. A creature, a life held in my hands, as if it were something priceless, something outside of this world. Sitting on my heels in the sunshine, I held the little rabbit, thinking these were the happiest moments of my life. I don't know how long I held it in my arms—twenty minutes, a half hour. Finally, I put the rabbit back in its cage, pushed the carrot under its nose, and locked the door. I watched it nibble. After awhile, it stopped and watched me.

When I got back to the trailer I was surprised to find the doctor still there. He and my mother must have a lot to say to each other.

A few weeks later I stopped at the library on my way home from school. They gave me a library card and let me check out a book called *Peter Rabbit*. I hurried home and read the book to Bunny Boo, holding him in my lap, where he seemed content. Even fell asleep. Must have been the sound of my voice, or maybe he didn't think Peter Rabbit was a very good bunny, the way he kept stealing everything.

One Saturday afternoon in midsummer I put on my shorts and sat barefoot and cross-legged on my bed with my red monkey. I was reading *Just So Stories* by Kipling when I became aware of my mother. She stood in front of me in her fancy blue taffeta dress. "Going some place special?" I asked.

"Yes. The doctor has invited me to a party at the San Simeon Ranch. It's owned by William Randolph Hearst. I want you to go with me."

"Why?" I asked, not knowing anything about the ranch or William Randolph Hearst.

"Well, it's a big place. Some folks call the house a castle."

I scooted to the edge of the bed. "Can I explore it?"

"No, but it has a pool, so you can go swimming with the other children."

"Who are the other children?"

She sighed. "The children," she said with exasperation, "are the ones who belong to the parents at the party."

"I don't want to swim with them," I said. "I'd rather stay here."

She grabbed my arm, yanked me to my feet, and snapped, "You can't stay here. You're the reason I'm going."

"I thought you were going to the party with the doctor."

"I'm meeting him there," she said, her voice shrill. "Nobody's supposed to know. Now put on your socks and shoes, grab your swimsuit, and get into my car."

Off we went in Mother's Chevrolet coupe. I hadn't been in the car since Spring, when I traveled from San Francisco to King City. I was glad it was daylight, because the back road over the Santa Lucia Mountains to Hearst's castle was narrow and winding.

The doctor was waiting for Mother on the front steps. Although it didn't have parapets and towers and a moat like castles I'd seen in pictures, it was huge. I felt small and unimportant.

There were seven children swimming and thrashing about in a large pool. They all seemed to know each other. One of three servants standing guard asked me, "Do you want to change into your swimsuit?" I said, "No, I'll just dangle my feet in the water." I took off my shoes and socks. He held them by their edges as if they were filthy and asked me to follow him. He led me into a shower room, gave me a bar of soap and said, "Sit down on that bench and scrub your feet." He placed my shoes and socks and my wadded-up swimsuit in a nearby locker, turned on a hose, and watched me wash my feet, not turning off the water until I had cleansed away every speck of dirt.

I hadn't dangled my feet more than ten minutes, when a bell sounded. The children in the pool splashed out and into the shower rooms—boys in theirs and girls in the one where my locker was. Getting up my courage, I asked the girl who came out of the shower first, "What happens now?"

"Dinner, of course." She looked me up and down. "Don't you have a dress to wear?"

"No. "

"What a shame!" She opened her locker, took out a flowered print dress and tossed it to me. "This might be a bit big for you, but it'll make you feel less conspicuous."

"What about you?" I said. "What'll you wear?"

"Oh, I've got another one. That's an extra dress I keep here."

The girl was a foot taller than me. The dress was *way* too big. But after I put it on, she took one look, laughed, and brought a long silk scarf out of her locker. She tied it around my waist and pulled the skirt up under it. "There," she said. "Not bad. By the way, my name's Miranda. I gather this is your first time here. Sit beside me and I'll fill you in about the place."

We children sat at a table made of one large slab of wood in a room that looked out at the pool. I don't know where the parents were. It was a delicious dinner of lamb stew, fruit salad, and chocolate cake with ice cream. It was the best meal I'd had since I left San Francisco, and Miranda sure helped me out.

To celebrate my eighth birthday, Mother made me a beautiful, ankle-length, pink silk dress with lace netting over it. She hired the cook at the hospital to make a big cake and rented a large room off of the lobby at the swanky El Encanto Hotel, where all the business men and rich folks stayed. Mother came to my classroom to invite all 31 boys and girls to the celebration. "Don't bring presents," she told them. "I don't have enough room to store them."

As my birthday neared, my excitement grew until I could barely concentrate on my school lessons. The stone-faced math teacher, Miss. Kentzel, caught me passing a note to Daisy Mae Wong. Her family, the only Chinese folk in town, owned a laundry shop on Broadway. Daisy Mae was shy to the point of not joining in any games at recess. I think she felt as if she'd come from another planet.

Miss Kentzel said, "Barbara Jane, have you finished the problems in your workbook?"

"No."

"Would you prefer to stay after school to finish?"

"No."

"Then I strongly suggest you concentrate on your math problems rather than..." Miss Kentzel snatched the note from Daisy Mae's hand. "Passing notes like this." She held it up and read out loud what I'd written. *"Don't be shy, Just come."*

With a squeal, Daisy Mae hid her face in her hands.

I jumped to my feet. "Miss Kentzel, now you've done it."

"Done what?" thundered Miss Kentzel, waving the paper at me.

"You've embarrassed Daisy Mae. Now she won't come to my birthday party."

Miss Kentzel wadded up the note and threw it into the wastebasket. "You silly child, they were your words."

She stalked behind her desk and plopped down in her chair. A poop echoed through the room, accompanied by a bad smell wafting past my nose in the second row. Obviously the sound and smell had come from beneath Miss Kentzel.

Everyone tittered.

"Back to work," snapped Miss Kentzel, grabbing her pen and writing something that appeared to be terribly important.

On October 25th, my birthday, I rushed home from school and changed into my beautiful pink dress and shiny black, patent-leather shoes. I was a fairy princess, waiting for my carriage. The doctor drove Mother and me down to the El Encanto Hotel in his fancy

Bentley car. Some of my classmates already were waiting in the lobby.

It was a wonderful time with no parents around. We ate cake and drank pink lemonade. Mother hadn't left any instructions about what we should do after that. She was always more interested in setting up a beautiful picture than putting life into it. I got the idea of sweeping out of the room and into the lobby with everyone following me. We all fought for seats and giggled. A few minutes later I stood up and swept out of the lobby and back to the room with all 31 followers. Once more we fought over seats and giggled. When all were settled, again I stood up and led the charge to the lobby where we repeated the process, making more noise. And then, back I flew to the room with my entourage following. It was on our third appearance that the hotel clerk charged out from behind the front desk and herded us back into the room, shouting, "You rented this room not the hotel lobby." He locked us in, only opening the door when parents arrived to pick up their children.

Meanwhile, inside the room the boys threw chunks of cake at the girls. Daisy Mae hid behind the table. I fell down and tore the lace netting on my dress, and Jackie Burns, the best looking boy in class, took mouthfuls of lemonade and sprayed them at me. By the time Mother arrived, the room was a mess and my fairy princess dress was ruined. Mother pressed her lips together and muttered, "I should've known you'd do something like this."

"I'm sorry," was all I could think of to say.

My favorite school teacher came in once a week to teach art. I forget her name but she was tall, hair softly waved around her face, and she always wore a sort of filmy dress. She floated around the room, adjusting her glasses as she looked at our drawings, murmuring, "Um, nice," or "Well done," always something positive.

I also liked our science teacher—as different from the art teacher as a chickadee is from an eagle. She always wore a stiff-collared white shirt and a black skirt, her hair pulled back tightly in a bun, and she charged into the room with an arm full of books, breathless as if in pursuit of something important. She came in once a month and taught all morning. Although she was intimidating, she was full of wonderful knowledge. We listened with rapt attention.

The teacher we all disliked the most was Miss Kentzel, the stone-faced math teacher. Jackie Burns was sure she wore a wig. He said he had heard that once her wig fell in the wastepaper basket. We had a good laugh about that.

On a particular morning before Miss Kentzel came into class, Mutsy dared me to write on the blackboard *I love Miss Kentzel.* I had just finished and was running back to my seat when Miss Kentzel walked into the room. She marched to the front and erased what I had written. "Barbara Jane," she said, "stay after school and write 100 times what you just wrote on the blackboard."

I stayed and wrote the words 100 times. She took the paper from me and then said, "Why did you write that on the blackboard?"

The sadness in her voice surprised me. "Someone dared me to do it," I replied.

She cleared her throat. "It isn't always a good idea to take a dare."

"I know."

"You may go now."

Bigger problems for me began the night I started a fire in the trailer. I didn't do it on purpose, although Mother thought I did.

"You don't like living with me. You'd rather live with your grandmother."

"No," I lied.

"You turned on the electric heater and threw my blanket at it."

"It didn't happen that way," I insisted. "I sat too close to the heater. Your blanket caught fire."

She shook me by the shoulders. You planned the whole thing."

I broke away from her and ran to my bed. "I didn't plan it," I cried. "I woke up and you were gone."

"So, you took the blanket off my bed."

"I was cold. I wrapped it around me and turned on the heater."

"Why didn't you use your blanket?"

"I don't know. I saw your blanket and grabbed it."

With a snort of disgust, Mother returned to sweeping up the ashes at the other end of the trailer while I lay shivering, hugging my red monkey, my blanket pulled over my head.

I heard Mother say, "Lucky an orderly was resting behind the hospital."

I knew I was lucky. If he hadn't seen the flames when I ran out of the trailer...if he hadn't put out the fire by smothering it with Mother's mattress...the whole trailer might have burned up.

The next bad thing was the disappearance of Bunny Boo. The doctor thought I hadn't fastened the lock when I left my pet for the last time. I knew I had locked it. I always double checked. Mother thought one of the really poor people who lived in King City stole the rabbit for a good meal. That idea horrified me. How could anyone steal my beautiful, soft, furry, white bunny, kill it, and eat it?

For many days I came home from school and hunted all over the neighborhood. Knocked on doors. Asked people. Nobody knew anything. One thought haunted me. Had my mother unlocked the cage and let Bunny Boo go?

However it happened, my dearest, huggable, living pet was gone forever.

An even worse event occurred in the middle of the second summer we lived in King City. I was sitting on a bench in the hospital side garden, making hollyhock dolls. How I do that is pick a hollyhock bloom and turn it upside down so the bloom looks like a full skirt. Then I pick a bud and insert it on top of the skirt for the head. I had a lineup of five dolls with differed colored skirts when one of the nurses came out of the hospital to eat her lunch—a sandwich in a paper bag. She admired my dolls. "You're a clever girl," she said. "Would you like one of my gingersnap cookies?"

"Sure," I replied. "I love gingersnaps."

She handed me one.

"Thanks," I said.

She nodded and smiled. "You're the young lady who lives with Virginia in the trailer back there." She waved at the area behind the hospital.

I'd never been called a young lady. I liked it...liked her...her smile and her cookie. "Yeah that's me," I said.

"How do you like living in a trailer?"

"Not very much. It's kind of small and has no windows."

"Too bad about no windows. Nobody can see what's happening in there."

"Not much to see—oh, you mean the fire. Yeah, a window would've helped. That man could've seen the blanket the minute it caught fire."

"Right," said the nurse. "The fire." She wiped her mouth with a napkin and stuffed it into her paper bag. "Sorry you lost your Easter rabbit."

I nodded. "Wish I knew what happened to Bunny Boo."

She nodded and cleared her throat. "Did the doctor give the rabbit to you?"

"Yeah."

"Why?"

"I don't know. Maybe to give me something to do while he and my mother talked."

"Probably." She leaned toward me and whispered, "Did they meet very often?"

I arranged my hollyhock dolls in a single file. "I'm not supposed to talk about their meetings."

"That's OK. You can tell me," she said.

"Promise you won't tell anyone."

"I promise. How often did they meet?"

I looked around to make sure nobody else could hear me. "Just about every afternoon until I lost the rabbit."

She reached over and patted me on the arm. "Every afternoon? And you think they just met to talk?"

"I guess so." I swallowed hard. "Once I saw him kiss my mother. But that was only once."

"Did you know," she said standing up and brushing crumbs off her white uniform, "that the doctor is married?"

Again I swallowed hard. "I didn't know that."

"Thanks for the information." She walked toward the side entrance to the hospital.

I called after her, "Remember, you promised not to tell."

She kept on walking without looking back.

I had a sinking feeling that trusting her had been a mistake.

And it was—a terrible mistake.

Mother was fired. I figured it was because that nurse broke her promise not to tell. The following day Mother didn't come back to the trailer till midnight. Didn't get undressed. Just hunched up in her bed, crying.

I felt awful. Didn't know what to do. After a bit, I went over and patted her on the head. "I'm sorry," I said, trying to keep my voice steady, "I'm sure you can find another job."

"You don't understand," she said, pushing my hand away.

A few days later I was moved into a room in a lady's home. Can't remember her name. I think she rented rooms. That night my beloved Bamover arrived. Mother had called her, and she took the next Greyhound bus to King City. She gathered me into her arms as I sobbed out everything I'd done wrong.

We didn't see Mother for a year. Where she went I have no idea. Many years later I learned that the night she came back late to the trailer, crying. The doctor had given her an abortion and tied her tubes so she couldn't get pregnant again. Even if she'd told me why she was crying, I wouldn't have understood.

We stayed at the lady's house for two months. A door away lived a big Chow dog with purple lips. Every morning it ferociously chased me the two blocks to school. In the afternoon when school was out, the dog was always tied to a stake. It strained at the leash, barking as if it wanted to eat me up. I thumbed my nose at it and made a bunch of funny faces. After a week of having to run for my life, I'd had it. The first Monday morning of the second week, I sneaked out the back door and took another route to school. When I came back in the afternoon, the dog took one look at me, closed its eyes and went to sleep. Guess it figured I was no longer a threat to the neighborhood. As for me, I kept my part of our unspoken bargain. For the rest of the time we lived at that lady's house, I walked the extra blocks to school and, on my way home, I made no funny faces.

While we lived there, I caught a bad cold. Grandma made me drink lots of liquids and put cold compresses on my head. One night I ran a temperature of 103 degrees. I'll never forget that night because I had the worst nightmare of my life. Huge fire-breathing demons with horns and faces like that awful nurse came after me. I jumped out of bed. Holding my pillow as a shield, I ran around the room, dodging flames, screaming for help. It took an hour for Grandma to calm me down and convince me that it was only a dream. I have only two memories of my time at that lady's house: the ferocious Chow with purple lips and that horrible nightmare.

Grandma found us a small two bedroom house in Kirk's Court for $20 a month. It was on the southern outskirts of town, across from the school's gravel playground. I think of our three years there as my good times in King City. Sure, we were poor. My father sent $50 a month child support. Once a week I wrote a letter to Granddaddy Hunter; he always sent a dollar in with his reply. And every August Mother sent six dollars to buy me a new school outfit—shoes, socks underpants, and a dress with a deep hem that was lowered as I grew taller. For the first two years that was all the money we had. But food was cheap then. A loaf of white bread cost only eight cents, and we could buy four cans of tomato soup for twenty-five cents.

At the town's northern entrance, just before the bridge over the Salinas River, a sign on an archway touted King City as *The Pink Bean Capital of the World.* Lots of bean fields surrounded the town. A sack of dried pink beans cost next to nothing. Grandma often had a pot of them cooking on the stove. Being poor wasn't such a big deal. These were Depression years. Everyone was poor. Occasionally a tramp—what Grandma called "an out-of-towner, passing through"—would appear at our back door asking for food. Grandma would fix him a peanut butter and jelly sandwich. He'd sit on the back steps eating it. Then he'd wash his hands and take a drink from our garden hose and leave, never seen again. People in King City went on with there lives, making the best of it. Most important to me, I had the care and love I needed.

Kirk's Court consisted of five homes. Three were at the front of the property, along the street—our small two-bedroom; a larger two bedroom where a single lady lived; and an even larger three-bedroom, the home of the Kirk family. Behind us were two one-bedroom houses occupied by single men. Across the back of the lot were four garages, two on either side of a fenced in yard where one of the men kept Spot, his dog, a fox terrier that I visited and played with every day. The Kirk's home had a separate driveway to their garage. They were the only Court inhabitants with a car. The rest of us used our garages as storage units. At least I think that's true. I never saw any of the other garages open, but we kept four steamer trunks in ours.

We had a pint-size backyard as did the single lady. However, she grew vegetables in hers, while we let nature take over among the marigolds, Shasta daisies, nasturtiums, and a sturdy caster bean bush. The single lady told me that castor beans were poison. Even the leaves might be poisonous. I stayed clear of that bush.

One summer morning, without any warning, our tiny backyard sank down two feet. Grandma called the bank manager—the only important person in town she knew. He sent over an official, who measured the hole, took notes, muttered, "tisk, tisk," and went away. The next day a truck arrived, and six wheelbarrows full of dirt were dumped into the hole. Grandma asked if there was a charge for the dirt. The man shook his head and left. We never did find out what caused the sink hole. The single lady thought it might have been the Salinas River, which she claimed was "the largest underground river in the world." Whatever the cause, next spring the marigolds, Shasta daisies, nasturtiums and the poisonous castor bean bush grew better than ever. So did the weeds.

Our house was the only one in the Court with what Grandma referred to as "a front lawn." It was barely large enough to turn around in. Even so, Grandma was proud of that patch of crabgrass. Every summer evening after supper when the usual afternoon dust-swirling winds had died down, Grandma would be out with her hose hand watering the lawn until it was too dark to see. Then she would come inside and join me listening to the radio. I loved Little Orphan Annie and the Phantom Pilot Patrol. I sent away for an Orphan Annie secret badge. When certain numbers and letters were dialed on the badge, you got a message from Annie herself...a hint about the next program... such as *Sandy scares burglar away*. Sandy was Annie's dog. Sure enough, on the next program Sandy let out an "arf" and the burglar fled. I also sent away for a Phantom Pilot Patrol button so I could be a part of his patrol.

Grandma liked to listen to Ma Perkins and Gang Busters. We both listened to Major Bowles Amateur Hour. I wrote a poem about it: *I wonder if when I reach the Great Beyond* will *I hear, "All right, all, right" or will I get the gong,* Grandma sent the poem in to the show, and Major Bowles read it over the air. The audience laughed. I was proud; I had made an impression.

A few weeks after we moved into Kirk's Court, the Kirks moved out and rented their house to the Bridges, a family with two girls: Frances, called Mutsy, my age, with a determined jaw, and Sigor (never knew her real name), two years younger, slightly blond and very shy. We hit it off as playmates. When we climbed the tree out by the sidewalk, I was Tarzan, Mutsy was Jane, and Sigor was our ape child. When we played Cowboys and Indians, I was the Indian Chief, Mutsy was the Sheriff, and Sigor was either my squaw or the sheriff's wife.

We got into trouble when I was a doctor, Mutsy my nurse, and Sigor stood around watching. It all started the afternoon four-year old Charlie from up the street wandered into Kirk's Court. We decided to use him as our patient. What we really wanted to find out was what made him a boy. We took him into our garage and had him take his pants off and lie down on one of the steamer trunks. The week before we girls had closed our garage door, and in the darkness used a flashlight to examine each other's private parts. We could see that we were pretty much alike. When we studied the little boy, we saw something different. He had this tiny, loose thingamajig hanging down where his hole should be.

We were in the midst of our examination when the mother of the boy turned up. "What are you doing to my son?" she shrieked. We scattered like frightened pigeons, I to my house, Mutsy and Sigor to theirs. The outcome was that Mutsy and Sigor couldn't play with me for a week. I was devastated.

It was around that time that I found an imaginary playmate, Betty Jane. Downy, my imaginary playmate in Maine, was gone, left in a tree on the island. Betty Jane was someone I could go to for advice. We'd have conversations like, "Betty Jane, what did I do wrong?"

"You shouldn't have told Charlie to take his pants off."

"How else could I find out that a boy is different?"

"Was that important to you?"

"Yes."

"Then, you should've shut the door and used a flashlight."

Grandma listened to most of our conversations, but she never made a comment about them, although there were times, such as when I didn't want to take the garbage out, that she would say, "Go have a talk with Betty Jane."

And of course, Betty Jane would tell me, "Don't be a bad girl, Barbara. Take the garbage out right now."

Usually I followed Betty Jane's advice.

One afternoon, after school was out, Jackie Burns and his younger brother, T-Bone—have no idea why he was called that—sauntered over to Mutsy, Sigor, and me...we were on the swings... and he said, "Want to share an adventure?"

"Sure," said Mutsy.

I was suspicious. Why'd he want girls rather than boys? "What sort of adventure?" I asked.

"Somebody left one of the auditorium windows open. If we climb the tree next to it, we can get in and have some fun."

"Why don't you get the boys you play with? Why us?"

"They'd rather play ball." He fidgeted with his belt buckle. "Besides, I've seen you girls climb. You're good."

Mutsy said, "Let's do it."

It wasn't an easy climb, but we'd played Tarzan enough to make it.

Inside, we dropped about six feet to the floor of the empty auditorium.

We ran up onto the stage and started to whoop like Indians. The hollow sound of our voices was great. Not sure which one of us got the idea of taking the gravel out of the potted palms and throwing it up on the stage. It sounded like a rain storm. We were in the midst of throwing more gravel up when we heard the front door to the auditorium crank open.

"Someone's coming," cried Jackie."

"Hide in the bathrooms," yelled Mutsy. She jumped off the stage and led the way followed by Sigor, Jackie and T-Bone. All except me. I froze on the stage with a hand full of gravel that piddled out of my hand with a shushing sound.

A man's voice boomed out, "Who's in here?"

Too late to head for the bathroom. I rushed to the back of the stage. Where could I hide? A ladder, attached to the back wall, led up into the rafters. I clambered up. Below me the school janitor appeared—a nice man in other circumstances. He often gave lemon drops to us. Now I hid in the dimness of the rigging and didn't dare move.

He switched on the lights. I watched him sweep up the gravel on the stage and dump it back into the potted plants. He then went into the bathrooms and I heard him say, "Mutsy and

Sigor, you two get out of there. Go on, go home." The front door opened and slammed. A bit later, he called, "Jackie and T-Bone, are you in on this? Get, before I sweep you into the urinals." Again the front door opened and slammed.

Grumbling, "Stupid kids," the janitor switched off the lights and left by the front door. A lock clicked.

It was getting dark. Slowly I climbed down the ladder and felt my way off the stage. The window was too high to reach. The front door was locked. Would I have to spend the night in this awful place? Nothing to eat. Not even a pillow. I'd have to sit in a chair and wait until morning. Who knows when the auditorium would be opened. Maybe not for days. I could starve.

Wait a minute. Grandma would miss me. She would call Mutsy's mother and ask if Mutsy was home. Did she know where I was? Mutsy would tell her I was locked in the auditorium. What would Grandma do? Call the principal? Call her banker friend? Call the sheriff?

Suddenly I remembered something. Even if the front door to the auditorium was locked from the outside, if you pushed the bar down on the inside you could get out. I dashed for the front door, slipped and fell. Broke open the scab on my knee that I'd injured playing kickball on the gravel at recess. Never mind the bleeding. I pushed down the bar on the door and it opened up. Letting the auditorium door slam shut behind me, I raced home, threw open the door to my house, and hugged my grandma.

Grandma said, "Where have you been? Why are you so excited? What happened to your knee? Playing kick ball again this late? Sit down. Let me put some mercurochrome on it."

As she tended to my scrape, I babbled out the whole story.

Grandma listened without a word. When I was finished, she laughed and said, "Pretty clever of you to climb into the rigging. Calm down now. It's all over. Here's a nickel. Go up to the corner and get yourself a snow cone."

And that's what I did.

The next day at school Mutsy and Jackie Burns were called to the principal's office. When they came back, neither of them would look at me. At recess I asked Mutsy what happened.

She folded her arms and glared as if I was her enemy. "Sigor and T-bone were already there," she said. "He told us how bad we were. Said if we ever did anything like that again, he'd tell our parents to put us in a reform school." She stuck her chin way out, gave me a withering look, and marched away to play kickball.

After school, I walked over to Mutsy and Sigor's house, hoping they'd forget I hadn't been caught in the auditorium, but Mrs. Bridges said her daughters didn't want to play with me. I pressed my lips together and went home to talk with Betty Jane. "Are they mad at me because I hid in the rafters, and they didn't?" I asked her.

"That's part of it." she replied.

"O.K., they're upset because they were called into the principal's office."

"And...?"

"They were threatened with reform school, and I wasn't."

Betty Jane nodded. "So, what are you going to do about it?"

"I'll go to the principal's office and confess. The worst he can do is threaten to tell my grandma to send me to a reform school."

"But she would never put you into a reform school."

"Right." I thought about this for a minute. "Maybe the principal wouldn't threaten me. Maybe he'd think I was brave to confess when I didn't have to. Maybe he'd congratulate me for coming to him."

"That's a good possibility," said Betty Jane. "Do it tomorrow."

I got up early the next morning. Ate my usual breakfast of five pieces of buttered toast, each dipped in a glass of tomato juice until the juice was almost gone. Drank the rest and took off for school. I didn't tell Grandma about my plan. I'd let her know when I came home with the good results I was sure would happen.

I tapped on the principal's door. A deep voice said, "Come in."

I walked in and stood in front of a big desk. In back of it sat the principal, his glasses down on his nose, his flowing white hair lit up by an overhead light. He looked like I imagined the Grim Reaper would look. Grandma had told me that someday the Grim Reaper would appear and take us up to heaven or send us down to hell, depending on how we led our lives. I took a deep breath and burst out with my confession, ending up with, "I'm sorry I did it. I'll never do such a thing again. I know you'll understand why I came to tell you I was involved."

He stroked his chin and looked down at me. "Guilt!" he boomed. "You came to see me because you were plagued by guilt."

"No, not really. I came because Mutsy was so mad I didn't get caught that she wouldn't play with me."

My first mistake was telling him he was wrong. Being honest was my second mistake. The principal rose to his full height and glowered down at me. "You will stand in the corner of the entry hall during morning and afternoon recesses." He pointed at the door. "Go, now!"

As I stood in the corner at morning recess, the students in my class pointed at me and giggled, Mutsy and Jackie Burns tried not to laugh but couldn't help themselves. At afternoon recess someone started a chant, "Barbara is a booby...Barbara is a booby..." I was humiliated.

What happened to my belief that my confession was an act of bravery that the principal would commend me for? That afternoon I stalked home from school and told Betty Jane I didn't want any more of her advice. When I told Grandma the story, all she had to say was, "I bet Mutsy and Sigor think you were brave."

Grandma was right. Mutsy and Sigor soon knocked on our front door and asked me to come out and play Tarzan.

The summer I was ten, Grandma and I took a Greyhound rip back to Washington, D.C. to visit Granddaddy and Grandmother Hunter. Granddaddy had sent the money for the bus fare. We couldn't afford sleepovers at hotels along the way. We slept in our seats, only getting off for meal stops or for a coach change. We always managed to get front seats so we could be first off for the bathroom and then first to order food. For dinner, I usually ordered soup and mashed potatoes and gravy. For lunch, we shared the cheapest sandwich, me with a glass of milk and Grandma with a cup of tea. For breakfast, I had four pieces of buttered toast and a glass of tomato juice. As I did at home, I dipped toast after toast in the glass until the juice was all gone.

When I wasn't reading one of the four books I brought along, I stared out at the scenery and took naps. Grandma often started conversations with a person across the aisle. And thus we crossed the country for about a week. It was more fun going to Washington than coming home, probably because we were starting out on our adventure rather than ending it.

Granddaddy Hunter picked us up at the Greyhound station in Washington. He told us that Grandmother Hunter's brother and his family were visiting from North Carolina. "But don't worry," he said, "You can have your old room. Mr. and Mrs. McDonald are sleeping on the upstairs back porch. Their two children – Anna Florence and Billy—are camping in the backyard."

Although Billy McDonald was eleven years old, he was at least six inches shorter than me. Obviously, he had just had a haircut...not a hair out of place. Somehow that made his green eyes stand out. For the two weeks I knew him, he wore the same pair of neatly pressed blue shorts with a yellow seersucker shirt, but they never looked dirty. I asked him how after five days he kept his clothes so clean, what with camping in the backyard. He told me that each night his sister—Anna Florence—checked his shirt for spots. If she found any, she washed them out and hung his shirt on a hanger in the tent to dry. As for his shorts, she carefully folded them up each night and laid them between his mattress and the ground tarp. "Sleeping on my shorts keeps them well-pressed," he said.

Anna Florence was fourteen and a bit on the plump side. She took good care of Billy, "Because," she said, "that's what an older sister ought to do."

Five days later, Billy said that when he grew up he planned to marry me. There's a photo of us at a picnic in Rock Creek Park. Billy and I sit on a picnic table bench. Billy looks at me as if I am his sweetheart; I appear a bit confused. The large bow clipped on the side of my straight hair gives me a lopsided look.

The two weeks in Washington went fast, with picnics and watermelon spitting contests, a visit to the Lincoln Memorial, and an afternoon spent climbing the stairs of the tall, skinny Washington Monument. In the evenings, as I did when I was four years old, I caught fireflies in bottles to watch them glow.

I wonder why Billy proposed. Perhaps by saying he wanted to marry me he was just being friendly. My Washington friend, Teddy—I kept in contact with her by letters after I left—wrote that it probably was because of my *vibrant personality*. It didn't matter why, because when he grew up he married somebody else.

I don't know where we got the piano, an old upright that was never tuned. It was in the spare bedroom on the inner wall next to the window. When I was ten, I started taking piano lessons with Mrs. Rianda who lived on the other side of town. Once a week I loaded my John Williams piano books into my bike basket and rode off for a lesson. It took me about a year to get to book three in the series.

Once we had a piano recital and I played Mozart's Minuet in G and also the base part of a duet with Mrs. Rianda. I was never as good as a nine-year-old boy who had big hands and ran all over the keyboard. My fingers were so small I barely reached an octave. Even so, Daisy Mae Wong came over and stood beneath the window to hear me play. She never came into the house...seemed too embarrassed to do that. She talked to me through the window, something like, "Play that piece again with the trills." And I did. Then she said, "That was good." And I beamed. I always felt I played my best for Daisy...better than at the recital.

Besides Daisy Mae, there was another shy girl named Sidley in my class one year. She came in the spring and never came back in the fall. She had a hard time with the lessons and wore the same dress every day. I had two. However, that included the dress from last year which had the hem all let out by April. I was embarrassed. Most girls in the class had three dresses.

During recess one day I told Sidley I'd help her with reading after school, but she said she had to get back and help her mother and father in the fields. They must have been one of those families who came in to weed the sugar beets. There were more beets now than pink beans, since sugar could be manufactured from the beets by Spreckles, a company north of King City. Sidley said she and her family came from Oklahoma. I wondered where she lived during the time she was here.

A family of Mexicans who worked the fields—a man, a woman and two grown sons—lived in a tin-roofed shack just south of the school yard. Mutsy, Segor and I used to throw rocks on their roof. I'm not sure why. Maybe we liked the sound or wanted to see if we could annoy the people inside. One summer evening we got a bunch of bigger rocks and started throwing them at the roof. A Mexican man burst out of the house waving a shotgun at us and yelling in Spanish. We dropped our rocks and ran away. That was the last time we pelted the roof. In late fall the Mexican family disappeared and didn't come back until the following summer. Where did they go in between? Mutsy thought back to Mexico; I thought they worked fields further south; Segor said she didn't know but was sure they went somewhere.

I knew we were poor, and I tried to hide it. I came home for lunch rather than eat my usual peanut butter and grape jelly sandwich at school. I was sure the other girls had much better sandwiches. On Fridays, when most of the students in my class brought in 25 cents for individual bank savings accounts, I announced I had another account to which I contributed—I had nothing. It got so bad that after our rent went up $2, then, by the end of the month our supper was often broken up soda crackers in a glass of milk or flour and water pancakes. I assured my Grandmother that it tasted great. I wondered what I could do to help.

One afternoon when Grandma was downtown, I took her box of sterling silverware, service for eight, over to our neighbor's house to see if she would buy it. She gave me $25 and then gave the silverware back, saying she was sure this was some sort of a mistake. Grandma was horrified that I tried to sell her silverware, one of the few things she had kept from her marriage to Compton W. Jones. She told me to give the neighbor back the $25. The neighbor said, "No, tell your Grandmother it's a gift. I appreciated having the opportunity to see such a wonderful treasure." That day I decided I would no longer sneak into the neighbor's vegetable garden and eat the tiny tomatoes she grew. She must have known I stole her tomatoes, because several weeks later she brought over a bowl of the tomatoes, telling Grandma, "I believe Barbara likes these."

I seldom went to the grocery store with my grandma, but one day I went, hoping I could talk Grandma into buying me a packet of Juicy Fruit gum. However, when Grandma bought only two potatoes, a quart of milk, and one small can of string beans, saying she couldn't afford to buy the larger can, I knew I couldn't ask for gum. When nobody was looking, I slipped a packet of Juicy Fruit into my pocket and walked out of the store without paying for it. When I got home, I pulled the gum out and showed it to Grandma.

"See what I got," I said, smiling at my cleverness.

Grandma didn't look happy. "Where did you get that?"

"I took it from the store."

"You took it?"

"I knew you couldn't afford to buy it."

"You wanted the gum, so you stole it."

I cleared my throat. "Well, sure." The word *stole* didn't sound good. Maybe I wasn't so clever.

Grandma folded her arms. "I suggest you go into the bedroom and have a talk with Betty Jane. Ask her what she thinks you should do."

I stomped off to the bedroom and plopped down on the bed. "OK, I stole the gum." I told Betty Jane. "So what?"

"How do you feel about it?" Betty Jane asked me.

"Lousy!"

"What're you going to do to feel better?"

"I could ask Grandma to take the gum back and say, 'My granddaughter took this by mistake.'"

"You could try that. Or..."

I thought about it for a minute. "Or I could take the gum back and slip it onto the rack when nobody is looking."

"Or..."

I sighed. "Or I guess I could take the gum back and apologize for stealing it."

"Which do you think is the right thing to do?"

Taking the gum back and apologizing for stealing it was the hardest thing I ever had to do. But I did it. As I stood before the owner, my face burning with humiliation, to my surprise he smiled and said, "Thank you, young lady. For being so honest, here, have a stick of gum."

Besides trying to hide that we were poor, I wanted everyone to think my grandmother was my mother. It was two years since Mother had visited my class. I hoped everyone had forgotten what she looked like. When she appeared one day to visit my class I was upset no end. What made it even worse, she had bleached her hair and came with a man who wasn't my father. At recess a group of girls surrounded me. There were lots of questions. I gave as few answers as possible.

"Who was that lady?"

"My mother,"

"Who was that man?"

I shrugged.

"Why aren't you living with your mother?"

"Because I live with my grandmother."

"But why?"

I shrugged again.

"Where does your mother live?" "Where does your father live?" "Do you miss them?"

Shrug. Shrug. Shrug.

"Your mother sure is pretty."

"So's my grandmother." I fled into the bathroom and burst into tears.

Our public library was only two blocks away. By age eleven, I was checking out at least four books a week and reading every evening after supper. I especially liked the dog stories by Albert Payson Terhune and any saga about the sea or adventures with horses. When I discovered Zane Grey's books about the wild west, I read every one the library had—thirty or forty of them. One that fascinated me was about a hidden valley reached only by a small opening. I was sure that valley was near King City and spent many weekends hunting for it over fields, near the Salinas River, even at the city dump.

It was almost dark one evening when I walked to the library to return four books and to check out more. I had almost reached the door when a man jumped out of the bushes and yelled, "Boo."

I screamed, dropped my books, and ran home. Out of breath, I dashed into the house and sank to the floor. "Man...in bushes." I cried. "He yelled, 'Boo.'"

By the time the sheriff arrived at the library, the stalwart lady from the front desk had captured the man. At my scream, she had rushed out and pulled him inside. She had forced him to sit down and explain himself.

"I'm sorry I scared the little girl," he said.

"Why did you do it?"

"Not sure. Maybe because she looked so serious, marching down the path with her books."

"Why were you hiding in the bushes?"

"It was a safe place," he answered.

That evening, the sheriff came over to our house. "Did he touch you?" he asked me.

"No."

"Did he expose himself?"

"What does that mean?"

"Did he show you his genitals?"

"What are—"

Grandma interrupted, "You know, the things that make a boy different from a girl."

I blushed. "Oh, those. No, he didn't show me anything except his face."

The sheriff led me out to his car to identify the man, who apologized for scaring me.

Later Grandma found out that since the man wasn't a member of the King City community, and the sheriff couldn't figure out what crime he had committed, he drove him to Salinas. He let the man off on the outskirts of town. "It's a bigger place," he told Grandma. "If he causes any trouble, they'll know what to do with him."

As for me, I was relieved to find the library books I'd dropped were back on the shelves.

Grandma and I went to church every Sunday. It was the Baptist Church on the corner a block away. We always wore our best clothes. Each Easter, Granddaddy and Grandmother Hunter sent me a fancy dress to wear for the whole year. Mostly they were pink organdy.

Early on I was baptized by the minister in a tank of water behind the pulpit. I had to take off all my clothes and wear a white sheet with a hole in the middle for my head. The minister told me to hold my breath and grasp his right arm. He put his left arm under my shoulders and dipped me down, saying, "I hereby baptize you in the name of The Father, The Son, and The Holy Ghost." I knew that The Father was God, and The Son was Jesus, but what was The Holy Ghost? Grandma didn't know either, although she guessed it might be an important angel. We were too embarrassed to ask.

Once, a heavy lady wanted to be baptized. In the middle of the dip, she let go of the minister's arm. She sputtered, thrashed around in the water, and knocked off the minister's glasses, giving him a bloody nose. Luckily, one of the ushers was nearby to help lift the woman out of the tank. Otherwise, The Holy Ghost might have taken her up to heaven.

Sometime while I was in the sixth grade—the last year we lived in King City—Grandma got the idea that we would read the Bible from the start to finish. When she announced this in church, the minister suggested that I give a report at each Sunday service about what we had read during the week.

We decided I would do the reading out loud each evening while Grandma fixed dinner. I'd never read anything in the Bible, although I'd often seen Grandma reading it before we went to church on Sundays. She kept it in the drawer of her bedside table. Anxious to get started on the Sunday evening after Grandma's church announcement, I brought her Bible into the kitchen and opened it up.

I started reading the creation story in Genesis. I got to the third verse, *And God said Let there be light and there was light.* I stopped and said to my grandma, "I'm confused."

"How so?"

"In my science class I learned that the earth goes around the sun, so why in the beginning was the earth in darkness?"

Grandma slowly stirred the pot of beans on the stove. "Maybe at first there was a covering over the earth, so we couldn't see the sun."

I nodded. Grandma always had an answer. I read on. When I got to the sixth day of creation and God made cattle, I stopped again. "What happened to all of the dinosaurs?"

"Well," said Grandma, "perhaps a day to God was many thousand of years." She dished the beans into two small bowls and set them down on the table.

In the next verse I read about God creating the first man in his image. I said, "Adam doesn't sound like the early man I read about in science class—he never lived in the Garden of Eden. He lived in a cave. This is all confusing,"

"Maybe the stories in Genesis are a metaphor," Grandma said.

"What's a metaphor?"

"Sort of a comparison—one thing to another."

'So, what's this compared to?"

"To whatever the real story is, I guess. Now, eat your beans."

I closed the Bible and ate my dinner.

By the following Sunday, we had read through the story of the big flood and the animals going two by two into Noah's Ark. At church, when the minister asked for a report, I stood at the front of the congregation and said, "All we've read in Genesis from the creation story though the Garden of Eden and up to Noah's Ark, well, I think this really didn't happen. It's just a bunch of metaphors."

A gasp rose up from the congregation. I noted stunned looks on the faces of people followed by a flurry of whispers. The minister cleared his throat and then spoke in a commanding voice. "Thank you, Barbara Jane. However, in the future we will be glad to hear from you only after you realize that the biblical stories are true accounts...sent to us from God."

And that was the end of my reports to the folks at the Baptist Church.

Shortly after that, I was playing kickball during school recess when I felt a pain in my right side below my stomach. I went ahead and kicked the ball. The next thing I knew I was in the hospital, waking up from having my appendix removed. That may have been why Grandma got a job as night nurse at the hospital. Since she had to get ready to go on duty before dinner, I helped fix the meals and didn't have time to read the Bible except on weekends when she had her nights off. We didn't make much progress with the reading, especially when it got to the chapters on lineage. They went on and on about somebody who begot somebody who then begot somebody else and so on down the long list of who begot whom, verse after verse, chapter after chapter. With Grandma working and many chores to catch up on the weekends, finally we decided to take a break from the Bible.

When Grandma went to work at 7:00, she locked the front and back doors for my safety and took the keys with her. Many times, I wanted to go out and play with Spot, the dog, or do other things. I unlatched the window screen in the bedroom and climbed out the window. As the days grew lighter with spring, I would stay out until 9:00. I never told Grandma about my nightly escapades. As I told Betty Jane, my imaginary playmate, Grandma didn't say I couldn't climb out the window. I wasn't hurting anybody. So, it was okay, wasn't it? Betty Jane wasn't sure. After two narrow escapes from danger, neither was I.

It was late spring, a Friday night, and I felt adult enough to slip out the window to visit the carnival that had come to King City for three days. I could have waited until Saturday and gone with Grandma on weekends when she had time off from the hospital. She had promised to let me ride the Ferris wheel and the Merry-go-round. I looked forward to that, but I wanted to see the carnival at night with all the bright lights and the excitement that came with being out in a crowd at night. I didn't have any money to spend, but that was okay. I just wanted to be there and see everything. After all, I was eleven years old; why not slip out and go to visit a wonderful place on my own.

I waited until it was dark, nine-thirty. Wearing my Sunday pink organdy dress, I climbed out the window and sneaked up the dimly lit street, past the Baptist Church, and the corner market, toward Broadway, the main street in town. Before I reached the two vacant lots where the carnival was, I saw the giant Ferris wheel, glowing against the night sky, and I heard the tinny music of the merry-go-round. I was excited and hurried ahead.

I mingled among the throng who ate cotton candy and snow cones, pitched balls for teddy bears, and sledge-hammered the scale to see how high it would go. I watched people go on the many different rides and listened in wonder to all the carnival noise.

I didn't see anyone from school...figured they would all be there on Saturday or Sunday. I caught a glimpse of Mrs. Rianda, my piano teacher, and hid behind the swirling teacups. If she saw me she would want to know why I was at the carnival at night by myself.

After an hour, I had seen and heard enough. I started home along the dark street. A car with two boys in it drove up behind me and one of them yelled, "Hey there, girlie, how about a ride?"

I walked faster.

The engine revved. "Need your arm twisted?" cried one of the boys, and I thought I heard the car door open and slam shut.

I burst into a run, crossed over to the next street to the Baptist Church. As I heard the car whip around the corner, trying to head me off, I ran behind the church and hid under a shed at the back of the parking lot.

"Where'd she go?" hollered one of the boys.

"Think she went behind the church," said the other boy. "I got my flashlight."

A light played across the parking lot.

"Don't see her," said one boy.

The light passed by the shed and then came back to shine in my eyes.

"There she is," shouted the other boy, "hiding under there."

Petrified, I tried to make myself as small as possible, hugging my knees and trembling, staring out at my tormentors.

For what seemed like an eternity, but probably was only a few moments, the light shone on me. At last one of them said, "Come on. She's just a kid."

"Yeah," said the other boy, "I thought she was older."

Off went the light. The boys got into their car and drove away. I scrambled out from under the shed and ran home as fast as I could. Still shaking, I was barely able to climb back through the open window.

It was a month before I had enough courage to climb out the window again. The Real Joy Theater, our local movie house, was having a Friday night special showing of a Frankenstein movie with Boris Karloff. The cost for teenagers was only 50 cents. Although I was only eleven, I figured I could pass for a teenager. It was a show I couldn't miss.

Clutching my ten nickels tied in a handkerchief, out the window I went. It was still dusk. I took the grassy vacant lot up to Broadway where the Reel Joy was. I took this back way to stay away from the streets. I didn't want to meet anybody I knew. They might question me about why I was out on my own.

Also, I was afraid I might get chased again by the boys in the car.

The movie was great, exciting, scary as the dickens. When I came out of the theater, still under the spell of Frankenstein, it was dark, not even a moon. The vacant lot looked scary. Maybe I should take the lighted streets home.

Don't be silly, I told myself. It was just a movie. I started walking onto the lot. A rustle in the tall grass ahead. I stopped. More rustling.

Frankenstein's face flashed across my mind. Was he out there waiting for me?

No. It was the wind. I started forward again. The rustling followed me. It wasn't the wind. The sounds were right behind me now.

He was after me.

I broke into a run. Slipped and fell. Scrambled up. Frankenstein was after me. He would kill me like he killed the girl in the movie.

Screeching, "No-o-o-o," I raced across the lot with the monster in pursuit. Breathless, shaking, weak, I reached my window. I felt his arms on my shoulders. With supreme effort, I hoisted myself up, tumbled inside, and fell onto the floor. My fingers were shaking so much, I couldn't latch the screen. I slammed shut the window and leapt into bed.

Where was my red monkey? Found it under my pillow, not so red anymore, the fur nearly gone from snuggling with it every night. It was my safety valve against anything that hurt. My rescue from all that was bad.

I pulled the covers over my head and, clutching my red monkey, fell into a fitful sleep.

By the time I was eleven and a half, I had two boyfriends: Junior Jones and Gerald Shackleford. Junior had an upturned nose and wore a perpetually dirty pair of shoes. Although his clothes were always clean, they needed ironing. He was so embarrassed when he came to visit me that, when Grandma asked him, "Do you like my Barbara?" he turned red and stammered, "Yes-s-s." Then he squirmed so much that he fell down in the street and squirmed some more. Grandma smiled and said, "Stand up young man. If you sit on the porch steps, I'll bring you a glass of milk and a piece of cake (She made a one-egg cake with chocolate frosting every two weeks. By the second week, which this was, the cake was stale.) While I broke my piece up in the milk and spooned it from the glass, Junior heroically ate his piece in two large bites. That was the first time I let him hold my hand.

Gerald Shackleford had a broad face and a mouth that was a bit too wide. His clothes were perpetually clean even though he, like Junior, often fell when stealing a base in kickball. It was amazing how he always looked neat and clean. I let him hold my hand, too.

We three went to the half-price Saturday matinee at the Reel Joy Theater every week during the summer because we had to watch the intermission adventures of the Phantom Pilot. He would do miracles and leave us with a cliff-hanger ending. Would his plane crash? Would the evil guy finally win? This was always followed by a Disney cartoon, often with Donald Duck doing crazy things that made us laugh. Then back to the main feature. One I'll always remember was *Boots and Saddles* with Gene Autry, the Singing Cowboy.

We each paid our own way to the theater. Junior sat on one side of me and Gerald on the other. I held hands with both of them. In those days that was as far as a girl went. I didn't even get a kiss from either one. That would have spoiled the relationships.

At the end of summer Mother appeared in my life. Again. We were surprised to learn that a few years ago she had married a pink bean and sugar beet farmer south of King City. His name was Mr. Gill. According to Mother, they had only lived together a few months before she took off for parts unknown. Now she was back to get a divorce because she and her pet parrot were planning on moving in with a man who had a large home on 23rd Street in Santa Monica. She insisted we were to move in with them. "Mr. Rianda wants to take care of us all," she told Grandma, who didn't believe her until Mr. Rianda appeared and said it was true. "If Ginny takes care of me, her whole family is welcome," he said.

I didn't like the idea of moving away from King City, away from my friends, and especially away from Spot, the neighbor's little fox terrier who lived in the pen between the garages at the back of Kirk's Court. Every day since we moved into our house I had made time to play with Spot. I would miss him terribly. As it got closer to September, and reality set in that we were going to actually move, I hugged my red monkey tighter and often cried myself to sleep

I stopped going to play with Spot. A week before the move I did something I've always regretted. It wasn't the right thing to do, and I knew it. I visited Spot for what I figured was the last time...coaxed him into the area behind the garages and the fence, so that nobody would see what I planned to do.

Spot brought the ball over and danced around, hoping I'd throw it for him to retrieve. Instead, I knelt down and hit him. Hard. Twice. He yelped and shied away. Then he crept forward and licked my hand. I yanked my arm back. Again I struck him. Even harder this time. He fell over with a louder yelp and disappeared around the corner of the garage. I closed my eyes and began to cry. As I started to stand up and leave, I felt a warm tongue lick away my tears. I reached out and enfolded Spot's trembling body into my arms.

How could I have been so uncaring and thoughtless to bring pain to a creature I cared deeply about? Betty Jane, my imaginary playmate, didn't know, and neither did I.

Two days before we were all set to leave...everything packed up except the furniture that would be shipped...the neighbor who owned Spot knocked on our front door and asked me, "Would you like to take Spot with you?"

"You mean you'll give him to me?"

"Sure. He means more to you than to me."

I was so excited that I gave the neighbor I scarcely knew a big hug.

Mother frowned and said, "There's no way a dog will fit in my car with all the suitcases and boxes."

But Grandma said, "If you can take along your caged parrot, surely there's room for a little dog."

And there was, nestled in my lap.

SANTA MONICA, CALIFORNIA

The drive in Mother's little car was cramped and seemed long, although it couldn't have been more than four or five hours. The caged parrot appeared to enjoy it more than the rest of us. Its remarks were said over and over. "Poly is a pretty boy" most often was interspersed with "Shove those beans up your ass," "I don't give a damn," and a maniacal laugh.

Each time the parrot spoke, Grandma frowned and her shoulders tightened. Mother, purse-lipped, kept her eyes on the road. The first time I heard the parrot's comments I giggled and Spot uttered a low growl. Soon, though, it became tiresome and then annoying. After awhile I wished the parrot would croak. By the time we reached Santa Monica, the tension in the car had risen to an explosive point.

At last we stopped at the 23rd street address. As we piled out of the car, Grandma said, "I don't want to ever see that blasted parrot again." Mother said nothing, but the way she grabbed the cage, I figured she must have thought the same thing. As for Spot, my little dog was obviously happy to relieve himself on a nearby bush.

The house wasn't as big as I had imagined. However it was elegant. It turned out to be two places: a one story, two bedroom in front with a one story, one bedroom behind it. In between the houses was a tropical garden— big leafed plants, lots of ferns and hibiscus and orchids of all colors—the perfect place for the parrot.

Mr. Rianda and Mother lived in the back house. Mother said we could each have a bedroom in the front house, but Grandma suggested that at first she and I share the bed in the largest bedroom. "This is a big change for Barbara Jane. She might feel safer." I was relieved to hear her say it, because the new situation frightened me.

"She's got to grow up," said Mother.

"Give her a week," insisted Grandma.

Mother raised her voice. "I never had any chance to feel safe."

"That wasn't my fault," snapped Grandma.

"Well, it wasn't mine," Mother yelled.

It was one of many arguments the two of them had about Mother's childhood.

As it turned out, we were there only five days. Mr. Rianda and Mother had a fight. Don't know what it was about, but he called Mother "a tramp," and she called him "a stupid old man." The next thing we knew we had to pack up everything and leave. One thing I was glad about. Mother left that *blasted parrot* with the *stupid old man*

In Santa Monica Mother found us an upstairs, one-bedroom apartment with a cot in the breakfast room where she slept. It was far from the elegance of the 23rd street home, but Mother said it was only temporary. Meanwhile, she got a job as a receptionist for the hair salon at J. W. Robinson's Department Store in downtown Los Angeles. I was enrolled in the local junior high school, and Grandma found the Baptist Church a few blocks away from out apartment.

Mother came home later and later each night. Most often after midnight, or as Grandma said with a frown, "After the bars closed."

Then one morning it happened. About 3 a.m. the doorbell rang, Spot barked. It was two policemen, lugging in Mother who had been in an automobile accident. Grandma shut the bedroom door, but I jumped out of bed, opened the door a crack, and listened. Mother was moaning. Even through the small opening, I could smell alcohol.

One of the policemen said, "She's drunk. Hit a telephone pole. Knocked half of her teeth out. She'll need a dentist right away."

Grandma said, "We're new here. Don't know any dentists."

"If it's OK with you, ma'am," said the other policeman, "I'll call one we often use."

"Please do."

The front door opened and closed again. I gathered he went out to the patrol car to call the dentist.

Mother kept moaning. I hopped back in bed and pulled the covers over my head.

An hour later Spot barked again. The dentist had arrived. Through the door crack I heard him tell Grandma he'd have to take out Mother's top teeth and dig out the roots. "The only good thing is she's so drunk she won't need an anesthetic."

Slipping deep down under my covers, I desperately wished I hadn't left my old, beat-up, red monkey on the pile of stuff aimed for the King City dump.

With a swollen mouth and no upper teeth, naturally Mother lost her job at Robinsons. She did get a set of false teeth made. Don't know how she paid for them; Grandma thought maybe her bar friends "kicked in."

What Mother did next upset Grandma no end. Mother wrote to the Nursing School that Grandma graduated from and Mother didn't. In her letter she asked to see what a graduation certificate looked like. When one came, she ink-eradicated *sample copy* from the paper and filled it out as if she had graduated. Grandma said she could go to jail for doing that, but Mother didn't listen to her. Instead she bought a white uniform and got a job as a nurse at Douglas, the airplane manufacturer. On her first payday we moved into an old two-bedroom house with four steps leading up to a wide front porch.

Nobody ever questioned the phony certificate, nor did anyone ever think Mother wasn't a good nurse. And in spite of Grandma's worries, Mother didn't go to jail.

My first few days at Lincoln Junior High School were scary, not knowing anybody. Soon though I had two friends—Ethel Daugherty and Laura (forget her last name). When I spoke up in our homeroom class with correct answers to geography questions, suddenly all of the girls were my friends and even some of the boys.

At home I listened to the radio every evening, One of the programs I liked was Walter Winchell—"Good evening Mr. and Mrs. America, from border to border and coast to coast and all the ships at sea. Let's go to press." He was a gossipy sort of journalist. I got the idea of doing a Barbara Winchell program at school—"Good morning boys and girls of Mrs. Ahearn's seventh grade English class at Lincoln Junior High School and all the ships at sea. Let's go to press. Yesterday Joey Duncan hit a home run on the local baseball field. Look out Yankees. Joey's a fan of the Brooklyn Dodgers, and surely with all his talent he'll soon make the team and help the Dodgers take the World Series. Joey was overhead saying, 'Those bleep Yankees always win. Next year, mark my words, they're gonna lose.' Now a word from our sponsor, Ooodle Doodle Bath soap for your dog." Then Ethel came on and sang a little jingle, "Use Oodle Doodle to wash your poodle or any other doggie's noodle. Oodle Doodle you will find is very goodle for cleaning up the cullabaloodle that doggies leave behind." After that I returned with my latest press release, "Ava Garner gave a tremendous book report...."

Mrs. Ahearn let me give the Barbara Winchell report once a week for the three years

I was in her English class, and it was the one day of the week there were never any absences.

Marilyn and I became Girl Scouts when I was 13. It was fun working for the various badges, which were achievement patches you could win if you successfully completed the requirements for them. I got excited about seeing how many I could win, such as those connected to cooking, outdoor living, and hiking. Marilyn and I had an unannounced contest as to who could get more, until our scout leader informed us we should stop thinking about how many badges we got. What was more important was how well we did to win each badge.

One of our favorite Foot badges was when we walked up to Brentwood, which was a couple of miles above Santa Monica. At the time I was making a scrapbook about movie stars and had learned that a number of stars had homes in that area. One time we went to Shirley Temple's front door and I rang her bell. The door opened. Before we could say anything a smiling lady, wearing an organdy apron and looking like she was in a Temple movie, handed us two autographed copies of Shirley doing a tap dance. Then she curtsied and shut the door.

We figured she must have seen us coming and had a stack of autographed photos ready for distribution.

Another time we found actress Joan Crawford's house. There was a big wall around her home. We stood by the iron gate, wondering if we should climb over it. No, we decided. We might be considered burglars. Suddenly the gates opened, and a delivery truck swept through. We ran in after it. The gates clanged shut behind us. How were we going to get out?

Bravely we walked up to the front door, and I pushed the buzzer. A tall, thin, beady-eyed woman in a black dress opened the door. She looked like a character from a horror movie. In a haughty voice she said, "I told you on the phone, 'Deliveries are at the back of the house.'"

I said, "W...we aren't making deliveries. We're G...Girl Scouts."

Marilyn said, "We came to get Joan Crawford's autograph."

There was a long pause while the lady looked at us as if we were from outer space.

I said, "Sorry. We'll be happy to go. How do we get back through the gate?"

The lady shut the door and the gate opened.

We turned to leave.

The front door opened again. "Wait," called the lady. She held two pictures of Joan Crawford, her signature on both.

We each grabbed a photo.

Shouting "Thank you," we ran for the gate.

It clanged shut behind us.

The Baptist church was just five blocks away from home. The older Grandma got, the more religious she became. Realizing how much religion meant to her, I went along with it. I joined the Baptist Young People's Group. We met after the church service was over, sang songs, such as *Onward Christian Soldiers* and *Jesus Loves Me,* and ate lunch together. I made up little sermons and every once in awhile gave them to the congregation. Fred Judson, our pastor, was so impressed that he gave me a scholarship to the month-long Baptist Youth Summer Camp. There I was one of six campers entered into a sermon contest.

The day before the contest I was upset to learn that we couldn't use any notes. I needed mine to remind me about what came next. How was I going to stand up in front of everyone without my reminders? All day I kept going over what I was supposed to say. I couldn't get through my sermon without my papers.

That night I was number four in the contest. I sat on the stage, getting more and more nervous as my time approached. My name was called. I stood up and started talking like a zombie. I got through the first ten minutes, remembering what to say. Then I stopped. I couldn't think about what came next. The silence in the audience grew as I stood there in a panic not knowing what to do or say. Forgetting my sermon, I started singing, "Onward Christian soldiers, marching as to war, with the cross of Jesus going on before." and then switching to, "Jesus loves me. This I know, cause the Bible tells me so." I bowed and sat down to scattered claps.

I didn't win the contest, but I learned a lesson: be prepared for anything. This was even more knocked into me at the talent contest the following night. I had offered to play the piano for a singer. I forget the piece, but it was one I knew well.

When our turn came, we took the stage. I played an introductory chord and then started the piece. She began singing but in another key. I only knew it in the key of C. Obviously it wasn't what she was singing. We sounded terrible together. She sang louder with a horrified look on her face. I thumped the piece louder, hoping she could change to key C; she couldn't. I continued to play while she sang heroically to the end of the piece. At that point I jumped up from the piano stool and escaped the stage through the back curtain. For the rest of the time at the Baptist Youth Summer Camp if I saw her coming toward me, I ran the other way.

There were lots of fun things we did at the camp. We paddled canoes, took hikes, leaped into the water from an overhanging limb, and climbed a huge mountain. However, what I remember most about that month of camping was the horrified look on that poor singer's face and the overwhelming silence of the audience when I forgot my sermon.

When I got home from the camp, I found out that our landlord had divided our house in two. He took the back unit and rented the front one to us. This meant we had no backyard, no real kitchen, and no dining room or bedrooms. The front porch had been enclosed and two single beds put there. Beside the bathroom sink was a hotplate. Under the sink there were dishes, and in a nearby drawer, silverware. At least we still had the large living room with a fireplace.

The worst part of having no backyard was needing to let Spot out in the early morning without a fence to confine him. Grandma said he had barked at the boy on a bike delivering newspapers. The milkman claimed Spot tried to bite him. He refused to deliver our milk until we kept our "vicious" dog inside. So, until I came home, each morning Grandma put a coat on over her nightgown and took Spot out on a leash, which didn't make her happy. "Please, don't go away any more," she pleaded. Also, without the extra bedroom, Mother had moved in with someone who lived in nearby Topanga Canyon. Grandma said she probably was living with one of her bar friends. A lot had happened at home during the month I was at the Baptist Youth Summer Camp.

Mother soon got tired of working as a nurse at Douglas. Somehow in 1939 she got a leave of absence from the aircraft company. She found a job as a nurse on the SS Mariposa, a fancy English ship that carried tourists to islands in the South Seas. Since 1939 was the year that war broke out between England and Germany, the ship came back to Los Angeles in a convoy. That was the end of that job. I have a photo taken of Mother buying a grass skirt in Samoa. In that picture she looks healthy.

However, when she got home she claimed she'd caught pneumonia on the way to the South Seas. As a new member of the crew, she'd been dunked in the onboard pool when the ship crossed the International Date Line. She sued the steamship company and won a settlement. Don't know how much. I only know Grandma was disgusted that Mother had filed "a phony lawsuit."

Mother also talked the owner of the building where we lived into moving out of the back unit and allowing us to move in. Mother took over the big bedroom, and Grandma and I shared the double bed in the small bedroom. Grandma was happy to have a fenced backyard for Spot and a kitchen.

After a week of confinement in the backyard, early one morning Spot dug his way out under the fence. We heard him barking in his most ferocious way. I ran out in my pajamas and grabbed the dog. Unfortunately, he'd bitten a girl's ankle. Probably she had come too close to our front porch steps. The girl ran off crying. That evening the girl's father appeared at our door and handed Mother a hospital bill. He told Mother that unless she confined that "terrible creature" he would bring a law suit against her. As soon as the man left, Mother swooped up Spot and headed for her car. I pleaded, "Please don't take him away. I'll buy a muzzle for him. I'll tie him up in the backyard. Spot was only trying to protect us."

Mother didn't listen. She drove off with Spot and came back without him.

That was the last time I pleaded with my mother, and it was the last time I cried about anything she did.

After December 7th and the Japanese attack on Pearl Harbor, Mother became patriotic. She joined the Women's Ambulance Defense Corps of America. When there was a phone call with a yellow alert, which happened in the middle of the night about once a week, she drove an ambulance to the end of Santa Monica pier. I don't know what she was expected to do there, but she sat in the ambulance until the yellow alert was lifted.

Grandma was patriotic too. Twice a week she went to the Red Cross to knit long woolen scarves for service men to wear.

As for me, I was a fire watcher, which meant getting up on the roof during yellow alerts and watching for fires. I often fell asleep up there and Grandma had to call me to come down. I never saw a fire.

When I was 14, I got interested in boys and started having dates. Not with boys at school—

they never asked me out, although when I walked along the street, often a car full of them would drive by and whistle. My dates were with boys from the Baptist Youth Group. We met every Sunday after church. A fellow named Eddie was our leader. He would suggest where we should go. Often the destination was Hope Roger's mansion in Pacific Heights. She had a tennis court which could be turned into a volleyball court. We all played. It was there that I met Frank Jackson and Don Holden. Both were high school graduates, about five years older than me. They separately asked me out. We would attend a movie or go bowling. Usually we ended up at a drive-in where we always ordered cokes and French fries.

Don was the first boy to kiss me. The next day when I took the bus to school, I wondered if people would notice anything different about me. Would they know that I had been kissed? Nobody said anything. Nobody even looked at me. I guessed it didn't show. However, all day I felt a special glow—I had actually been kissed on the lips by a boy.

The glow didn't last long. I found out Don was also dating my friend Laura. He was probably kissing her too. Although Frank was from a small town in Idaho and not well schooled in the literary arts, he seemed more honest. He said he cared deeply about me. So his kisses meant something. I gave him a group of my favorite poems to read by Byron, Shelley, and Wordsworth. I also lent him a book I had just finished reading—*Don Quixote*—and suggested he should try to get better educated, which he promised to do just to please me.

I became interested in English literature because of Uncle Charlie. He wasn't really my uncle. He had been my father's best friend until he and my father (after his divorce from my mother) both graduated from George Washington University as engineers. Then they went off in different directions. My father turned to engineering radio broadcasts in Washington, D.C., including Roosevelt's Fireside Chats. He invented the automatic fade in, fade out, and went on to join the RCA team that invented color TV. Uncle Charlie became an engineer for Douglas Aircraft in California. Since my father wasn't nearby, Uncle Charlie took over as a father figure. Every Saturday from the time I was in High School until I graduated from college he came over to our house Not only did he introduce me to literature before I became an English Major at UCLA, he taught me how to play bridge and chess. He took me to my first opera—*Lakme*.

We sat in the top row of the balcony, the so-called peanut gallery. The opera was enchanting. When Lily Pons, sang the Bell Song, she hit the high notes so beautifully it just about stopped my heart. I became a life-long lover of opera because of Uncle Charlie.

In 1942 Mother joined the WAC (Women's Army Corps), going through basic training in Des Moines, Iowa. She couldn't have joined if Grandma hadn't taken legal custody of me, since one of the requirements was having no children.

A few years into her army career, Mother was attached to a psychiatric unit on Staten Island, New York. One of the patients struck Mother's back with a chair. Several bones were broken, and she had to have a body cast and remain on her back until healed. As a result, she had numerous body sores.

Grandma and I were given an Army permit for the train ride to visit her. At the time, hardly anyone not connected to the military could use the trains because of the large number of soldiers being transported.

It was an exciting train trip for me. I was the only single girl on the train and had all kinds of attention from soldiers, including attempts to kiss me whenever I left my seat to visit the bathroom. They vied for the opportunity to sit across from us in our regular seats or in the dining car. Grandma became known as the "bird woman" because of a large number of feathers on her hat. I was the "cute young lady" traveling with the "bird woman."

We spent a week visiting Mother. Grandma did most of the talking to her. I didn't have much to say except, "Hope you get well soon." What I remember most about the visit was going to a dance attended by Russian officers. I guess they were waiting for their units to call them home. At any rate, half way through the evening I was dancing with a handsome Russian when he whispered in my ear in broken English, "Must come to my room now." I smiled and pretended I hadn't heard him. He tightened his arm around my back and maneuvered me toward the exit. "Must go now," he announced.

I tried to push him away. "No, no," I cried.

"*Ja, ja,*" he shouted.

I didn't know what to do. I ended up kicking him in the shins. "No!" I repeated.

Immediately he let go of me, bowed and said, "Mistake." He left me by the door and hurried over to ask another lady to dance. I didn't wait to see what happened to her. I was too embarrassed. I returned to my room. When

Grandma asked if I had enjoyed myself, I said, "Sure. Russian men are good dancers."

The Army was the love of Mother's life. It gave her a sense of commitment...structure...the feeling of doing something good for her country. In 1945, although her back still hurt, she became the adjutant to General Telford Taylor at the Nuremburg trials. She considered it the high point of her army career. Several months after the trials were completed, she got a medical discharge and retired as a Captain from the WAC. When she died some 30 years ago, after five more failed marriages (seven altogether), she had a military escort on the train to her final resting place at Arlington National Cemetery.

There is much more I could write about my mother, but this is my childhood memoir. So back to when I was fifteen.

That was the year I entered Santa Monica High School (Samohi). I remember my Geometry Class with Mr. Crawford, a jaw-jutting teacher with squirrely eyes. I didn't do well with geometry except once when he gave us a hard problem to solve. I sat in the back of the room. I dug into the problem, going at it backwards and forward. To my amazement I got what I thought was the correct answer and dashed up to show it to the teacher, He looked at me, his chin sticking out further and said, "You couldn't have done this yourself. You must have copied it from someone."

"No," I protested. "I did it myself."

He said, "I don't believe you," He dismissed me with a wave of his hand. I was shocked. I returned to my seat, angry and flustered. At that moment a girl, who I knew was at the top of the class, came up to Mr. Crawford. He proudly told the class that she had found the correct answer. I ended up getting a C in geometry. I think that was the only C I got in my three Samohi years.

Frank Jackson joined the U. S. Navy when I was sixteen. We wrote to each other at least once a week until I met Milton (also sixteen) that summer at a beach party. I fell in love with him, and he said he felt the same way about me. I composed a letter to Frank, telling him I was in love with somebody else...I was sorry to have to tell him this...I hoped he could forget about me. I didn't mail the letter, not wanting to hurt Frank. After two letters from him, asking why I hadn't written, I heard no more. I was so deeply in love with Milton I forgot all about Frank.

Milton was the son of the Ambassador to Chile. He was in Santa Monica visiting relatives during vacation time from the private school he attended in Santiago.

We saw each other every day...had telephone conversations each night before going to sleep...composed sonnets and read Shakespeare's plays together...hiked along the beach...played chess...made love in the front seat of his car—never going all the way.

This all happened until a week before Milton was to return to Chile. Then, suddenly he didn't call or come by to see me. I was frantic. Tried to reach him by phone. No luck. I cried much of the time. Grandma thought something bad must have happened to him.

The day before he left, Milton drove over to say goodbye. Without looking me in the eyes, he explained that all of his life, whatever he had loved had been taken away from him. "I let myself become too attached to you," he said with tears in his eyes. "I'll probably never see you again."

I was shocked. "Won't you come back to visit your relatives next summer?"

"No, they are moving to Chile."

"But, Milton, you can—"

He opened the front door to leave. "There's nothing I can do," he said, a catch in his voice. "This hurts too much." He ran out to his car and drove away.

114

I never saw or heard from Milton again.

A few months later I received a letter from Frank Jackson informing me that he was planning to marry his childhood sweetheart in Idaho. He had been corresponding with her all summer and realized she was *a better match for him than me.* I was indignant. So much for not wanting to hurt Frank's feelings. I tore up the letter that I wished I had sent when I wrote it.

Many years passed before I allowed myself to fall in love again. Never, though, was it as sweet as what I felt at sixteen.

Santa Monica High School (Samohi)

In school there was a dress code, white shirts and dark blue skirts for the girls, white shirts and dark blue pants for the boys. On Friday there was free dress. One girl always wore pink. She stood out, but I thought she looked strange.

I signed up for English and Journalism all three years. Mr. Kennedy was the teacher. After my first year working as a reporter for the weekly newspaper, he put me in charge of the Editorial page. Besides setting up the page with *Letters To the Editor*, I wrote an ongoing humorous piece about Chester, a fictional boy who had difficulties in school—what to wear, which class to take, who to ask to the end of the year dance. Nobody knew who I was.

However, when I ran for Senior Vice President the following year, in my qualifying speech before the student body, I mentioned that I was the Chester column's author. Not only did it get a laugh, but I think it was the reason why I won.

I loved the Journalism Class, especially learning how to run the old linotype machine. It was watched over closely by an old guy who set up the type each week for our newspaper. I thought for sure I would end up being a reporter like Brenda Starr, my favorite comic strip character. Mr. Kennedy gave me an A for everything I wrote.

My first year in college I returned to Samohi to visit Mr. Kennedy. It was after school, and he was still in his room, grading articles for the next issue of the newspaper. He stood up and said, "I wondered if I'd ever see you again."

I laughed. "You were my favorite teacher. I came back to see how you were doing."

He locked the room door. "I'm fine now that you're here," he said.

Then, to my horror, he grabbed me and gave me a passionate kiss. I pushed him away, ran for the door, unlocked it, and escaped. I ran out of Samohi and never returned. Someone I once honored had assaulted me.

I told no one about that meeting. Even now I don't like to think about it.

Westwood UCLA

I was able to afford school because tuition in those days wasn't expensive—about $29 a semester. I made money by marking catalog numbers in ink on the spines of books at the library. Also, I modeled suits at I. Magnin's department store during lunch hour.

Going to university was a mind-opening experience. It's not how much I learned, but how much my horizons were broadened.

Funny things I remember: An anthropology class with Dr Hoyer. He strode up and down the stage, with a tic in the side of his face, telling us about things like *Pithecanthropus Erectus* who was found on the Solo River in East Java in 1918 by Dr. Dubois. And then there was a philosophy class that made me think that maybe there wasn't a god. My grandma was worried and had me go see the pastor of our Baptist church-Fred Judson. He told me, "That's what happens when people go to university." Another course I took was creative writing. The teacher read my story to the class. Unfortunately, a couple of months after I took the course, he went up to San

Francisco and jumped off a building. I never understood why. Then I took a summer school class at UCLA from Clyde Tombaugh, who discovered Pluto. I figured out how to get to the moon in a rocket, and he gave me an A in the class. English classes really opened my mind- Romantic poets, Victorian, Shakespeare. I enjoyed a class on early novels, *Tom Jones* and *Don Quixote*. I took a Chaucer course and was able to go over to West Los Angeles to house on a big lot. It had an underground bunker where original copies of the *Canterbury Tales* were kept. It was so exciting to go over the pages with my gloved hands and actually see and touch what was done so many years ago. I didn't do well in French. But I did better in science courses, such as botany. I loved art history, which became a big influence in my life. I think in university you learn the world is a big place to explore. Education made me want to travel.

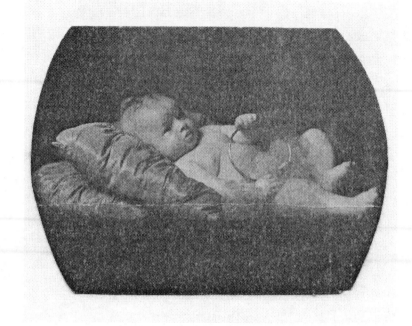

Newborn Barbara

Barbara at Six Months

Barbara at Age Four

Barbara Age Five

Barbara Age Seven

Snapshots of Barbara at Four

Barbara in College

Your Personal Memories of Barbara

(If you knew Barbara personally, feel free to jot your own remembrances of her on the following pages)